DRAMA AND EDUCATION

Drama
and Education

BRIAN WATKINS

Batsford Academic and Educational Ltd
London

In memory of my father, Jim Watkins,
whose legacy of loving kindness is
such a precious gift

©Brian Watkins 1981

First published 1981

Typeset by Typewise Limited, Wembley
and printed in Great Britain by
Biddles Ltd, Guildford, Surrey

for the publishers
Batsford Academic and Educational Ltd
4 Fitzhardinge Street
London W1H 0AH

British Library Cataloguing in Publication Data

ISBN 0 7134 3419 8 (cased)
ISBN 0 7134   (limp)

Contents

Acknowledgement

I gratefully acknowledge the influence upon my thinking of my students and colleagues as well as the authorities quoted in the book. My deepest thanks to them all for providing such an abiding and absorbing interest.

To Iain Ball I owe gratitude for his encouragement and for his share in the model, adapted by my good friend, Kevin Burns.

I thank Sarah Duchesne for teaching me so much about teaching, for her 'genius of feeling' and for the fun we've shared with the children of the Arden.

I thank Chrisoula Kapaka and the friends of Eubeoa for the loan of the tree and the well, and for the confirmation that learning springs from warm, caring, honest friendships.

My gratitude to Marguerite Lane who has typed the manuscript with care and concern.

Finally my thanks to my family for their abiding belief and support shown to me in their love and loyalty.

BW *Birmingham, 1981*

Introduction

The past decade has seen the severe decline of that provision made for drama in schools throughout the 1960s; the next ten years threaten its total extinction.

Some evidence for this depressing point of view may be seen in the virtual disappearance of Drama as a substantial contributor to initial teacher training and in the familiar non-replacement of specialist posts in secondary schools. Both result, as we are aware, from the problem of having to staff economically in the face of student reductions, falling rolls, and other resource cut-backs. Nevertheless, it has happened with a rapidity and such widespread incidence, that one could suppose that it reflects the lack of importance of Drama as a priority in Education.

Such suspicion might appear misplaced were it not that neither Drama, nor the arts in general, featured substantially in the Great Debate. Nor again in the survey 'Primary Education in England' by H M Inspectors, did the subject achieve more than barely a mention. Finally, whilst the emphasis on core curriculum continues to deny a place for the eduction of the feelings, it confirms that the greatest threat to the arts in education lies not in their persecution, but from their being simply ignored.

This book is an attempt to turn this tide of indifference by advocating that Drama is an indispensably powerful learning experience. Its unique balance of thought and feeling makes learning enjoyable, rigorous and obviously relevant to the whole realm of social life from which it takes its model.

Moreover, in that effective learning results from good teaching, this book will examine not only *why*, but also *how* the teacher promotes such activity. The result, it is hoped, will not be the so-called practical approach that recommends step-by-step instructions for the conduct of lessons, but a guide which will encourage the reader to relate the observations to his own teaching skills and local circumstances.

To encourage such confidence, however, there must be a clear understanding that when we talk about Drama we all mean the same thing. For I believe that it is the absence of such agreement that has led to frustration for many teachers attempting to use Drama, and for many more children who have been on the receiving end. Too often the resulting chaos in schools, already threatened by mounting pupil unrest, persuades the teacher to give up the struggle. They feel, quite justly, that what they or their classes get out of it is not commensurate with the amount of nervous energy it demands of them, a commodity already at a premium.

So the reader will find that this book starts with an attempt to define the nature of the dramatic process. This has been no easy task to undertake as a writer, nor should it be underestimated as a task for the reader, either. But it is hoped that the invocation of the Game, a familiar experience for us all, as an analogy, will encourage perseverance. Nor should these remarks be construed as apologetic, the sugar for an unpalatable pill. They merely support the view that it is pointless to proceed to an examination of the teaching of Drama unless we know what we mean by the term.

The introduction of the idea of Drama as Game is much more central to the book than just an illustration for a knotty argument. It appears throughout as a model that throws experience into sharp relief; the familiar made unfamiliar, and the unfamiliar rendered familiar. From such insights it is hoped to encourage understanding, assist lesson construction, and enable there to be analysis and evaluation.

Succeeding chapters maintain this focus upon the dramatic process but in its application to a variety of circumstances that contribute to the education of the individual or the community: play corner or theatre, tabloid or literary classic, the anger of the young or the memories of the old.

Lastly, and most important, because the teacher's role is seen to be crucial in the interpretation of all these situations, his contribution also appears substantially throughout the book. The assumption, common to all references, will be that as the teacher is part of the social structure of the learning experience, his effectiveness will depend upon his ability to operate meaningful relationships rather than pre-structured programmes.

1

The Game of Drama

The Problem

Drama teaching at all levels in our schools is in a state of confusion. This is not just because there is considerable disagreement about how to teach it, but because there exists no universally accepted idea of what it is or what is its purpose in Education.

There is a great danger that this situation is accepted by administrators as the inevitable vagaries of irresponsible artists. Their exasperated amusement could ensure that, at best, drama teaching in schools remains as an activity without any serious educational pretensions; at worst, that it is dismissed from the curriculum altogether. The problem for drama is not so simply explained, however, but illustrates the greater dilemma of our education system; the question of its responsibilities to a society that is itself racked with doubts about its values and its very continued existence.

Like other social institutions – Religion, Politics, Law and even Education itself, Drama has come to be regarded as a separate entity. This fragmentation of experience alienates ordinary people because in their exclusiveness these areas of what should be genuine community life become remote and mystified. This deterioration of the social process results in the divorce of these vital aspects of the life of the community from the common understanding and the will to participate.

That this fate has overtaken the drama may be seen in the immense and apparently irreversible falling away of popular support for the theatre. No longer obviously related to the affairs of everyday life, the theatre has come to be regarded by the large majority of people as the interest of an affluent and intellectual élite. And though the ready answer to this charge is that this lost audience, through television, now enjoy in their living rooms a range of drama such as never before available, if anything this has made the decline in understanding even worse. For the sharp distinction that is made by the television channels between its daily dramatic fare and the prestigious 'Play of the Month' reinforces the popular feeling that the arts

13

are the special province of the cultured. Conversely the westerns, gangster films, hospital fantasies and the parodies of ordinary domestic life are regarded more as palliatives for the end of the day than as relevant social commentary. This television medium that claims to have created a global village, by and large fails in its drama to give any recognisable or acceptable expression to the life of the mass of its villagers.

What makes this argument more than merely academic is the fact that it is against this inauspicious background that teachers who wish to use drama must work. They must recognise that their pupil's understanding and expectations will be conditioned by these television models which, though they may appear to represent real life, are in fact remote and unrelated to actual experience. Indeed the chances are that the class belong to that ninety-nine per cent of the population who do not support the theatre, the ways and means of which are literally less well known than the surface of the moon. In the absence then of a popular familiarity with drama as it is practised, we should avoid appearing over-specialized in an enquiry into its nature and purpose. To this end it would be better to avoid arguing the aesthetic exclusiveness of the subject and see more how it relates to other social experiences. In this way we might stand a greater chance of discovering the source of its power as a vital, expressive form. For as Raymond Williams points out in *The Long Revolution* (50): The arts, like other ways of describing and communicating, are learned human skills, which must be known and practised in a community before their great power in conveying experience can be used and developed. Human community grows by the discovery of common meanings and common means of communication.

Our major task, then, as teachers will be to develop these skills of describing and communicating in our classrooms and to assist pupils to rediscover how and why they can be used in an expressive form that is dramatic. But before we can do that, we have to agree about what we mean by drama; what did it mean to people in former times when it was a familiar and popular pastime?

The Game

Everyday expressions can often retain in the unconscious of the community the memory of former meanings and associations. So to this day we preserve in the familiar theatrical expressions players, playhouse, and the play, the relationship of drama to the whole world of Play and Game. This world, the anthropologist Huizinga points out, existed before culture itself and has accompanied and pervaded it from its beginnings up to 'the phase of civilisation we are now living in' (22). Furthermore it remains the same process it has always been, enjoyed by all ages and conditions of people in society. For the way it works, as we well know, is that it creates a world within the real world, a fictional existence governed by rules of our own making. The art of the dramatist is to relate these two worlds meaningfully to each other, and this, as we shall see, is achieved through the game of drama.

Nor is this the practice only of the artist in a highly civilised community. Primitive people, too, explain, control and venerate natural, supernatural and social phenomena through dramatic enactments. These communal celebrations, repeated, are the rituals that some claim give rise to Myth, the Epic and the Play – 'a secular conducted ritual revealed to non-initiates'.

Mimetic play satisfying 'the human urge for pleasure and recreation', at first imitated 'the external and tangible existence'. Later it was to become a thrilling yet awesome experience accompanied by 'fear', 'intensity' and 'concentration' designed to protect the community from the powerful forces of the supernatural. Later still, this struggle to survive by controlling Nature through representation; by becoming part of that powerful force, gives way to the rite in which 'the frenzy is spiritually directed: the soul departs the body in order to enter the godhead' – the true ecstasy.

So we can see how at the heart of the social process dramatic enactment has always been used as an expressive form. The severance of this activity from Play and Game is a more recent phenomenon marking that fragmentation of the social process mentioned earlier.

A definition

What do we mean, though, by a game? For although we have all experienced the playing, we seldom, if ever, stop to analyse what is happening. 'We might call it a free activity standing quite consciously outside ordinary life, as being not serious but at the same time absorbing the player intensely and utterly. It proceeds within its own proper boundaries of time and space according to fixed rules and in an orderly manner.' Thus Huizinga describes play in his book *Homo Ludens* (22), adding that the function of the play may be discerned from the two basic forms in which we meet it, either 'as a contest *for* something or as a representation *of* something. These two functions can unite in such a way that the game 'represents' a contest, or else becomes a contest for the best representation of something'.[1] Conflict and representation, then, are necessary elements of play and game, though it is made clear by Huizinga that by representation he does not mean mere show. In maintaining that it is the recreating of

15

something in a form that lends coherence to the original, he aligns this function exactly with that of drama. For the drama delivers up life as a unity rather than chaos through the 'representation' of human relationships in conflict or in crisis.

If we are clearer about what we mean by 'game', the next question asks what is the nature of this particular game, the game of drama, and how do you play it? The question does not have an easy or ready answer as the confusion in the teaching of the subject so clearly illustrates. Too often teachers have been given only very vague definitions, such as 'Drama is Life!' or 'Drama is as intangible as personality itself...'[2] Alternatively there have been disarmingly simple statements, like this one: 'Drama is action, movement, a form of physical, including vocal, expression. Therefore it has a near relationship with physical education...'[3] Such views, though not their intention, have created factions supporting dogmatically-held opinions of how drama should be taught. The rigidity of these positions has not merely divided drama teachers from each other, but also cut them off from a recognition of the real needs of their pupils. So if we genuinely desire the answer to the question posed earlier, then we must be prepared for a more exhaustive search.

The historical view

There is certainly no lack of evidence from theatre historians of the fact that at one time drama was regarded as a game. The Greeks, five hundred years before the birth of Christ, regarded the great drama festivals and the Olympic Games, the contest of physical prowess, as being essentially the same sort of events. Professor Wickham in his *Early English Stages* and Kolve in *The Play Called 'Corpus Christi'* demonstrate the synonymity of drama and the game through Medieval and Tudor times, right up to the Elizabethan and early Jacobean periods. As a game the drama depended upon a formal order, for without it 'progress within the game and pleasure from a game are alike impossible.'[4] And the order was inviolate, fines were imposed on those who broke the rules of 'ye game on corp's xxi day'.[5] The reason for this seeming over-sensitivity was that what the action of the play represented was regarded as being the truth. The play 'sought to pattern human experience, to give to the history of men an order that would reveal its meaning.'[6] Again we see the over-riding concern with the need men have to perceive a meaning in their lives which in turn brings order to the conduct of their daily affairs. In the drama we see a model of those affairs, selected in such a way as to show the consequences of breaking the order and destroying the values that represent social reality. This game, then, is about the hows and the whys in the way men lead their lives.

The uniqueness of this way of looking at life lies in how the game is played. For the players are, at one and the same time, people other than themselves, deeply involved and absorbed by the traffic of their affairs. Yet these same players are also supremely themselves, aware of the conduct and purpose of their portrayals. This is not a narrative experience that the players explore and communicate, but a dramatic one; a dynamic 'living through' of the encounters of persons whose relationships are affected by varying degrees of stress. It is, in fact, a model of the social interaction we experience everyday, but is selected and channelled to reveal its significance.

The sociological view

What do we mean, though, by 'the traffic of their affairs'; what exactly does the drama model? Here we may turn to an approach that has been made to the fundamental question of sociological inquiry, which is, 'How is social order possible?' What characterises this movement is that far from presuming that a social order exists naturally, they are amazed that it exists at all. This astonishment is the motivation for their studies, for it leads them to try to solve 'the puzzle, the mystery of how social order somehow emerges from the chaos and conflict predicated by the inherently meaningless.[7]

The reason why this school of thought is particularly relevant to our drama search is because it 'regards man as an actor who builds up his actions on the basis of his goals and of his continuing attempts to define and re-define the situation'.[8] They study the social world, then, from the point of view of the 'actors' who construct it. This way of looking at everyday social interaction as though it is conducted by players operating within a consensual structure, is to apply the game framework as a means of analysis. By formalising the process to this degree, it begins to resemble its model, the drama, much more closely, and to shed light upon exactly how the drama works.

Like the dramatist, these sociologists concentrate upon the encounter, the meeting of two or more people consciously acknowledging each other's presence and in communication with each other. They are able to recognise the situation in which they find themselves by reading the 'rules' of the exchange, this 'sanctioned orderliness arising from obligations fulfilled and expectations realised'.[9] The basis of the encounter is essentially linguistic, though extraverbal signals are also a vital factor in the progress of the action. Though apparently substantial, the structure of this interaction is in a sense transient, for it is always being built anew. It is in this way that men in life learn to define a situation and conduct themselves through it, by being aware of the ground rules that govern that situation as they appear in conversation. And though people involved in such encounters are not themselves aware of this structure, it is possible to study their behaviour with the aid of the game framework model. The participant certainly is aware of being in a problematic situation with which he is attempting to cope. He is conscious of his own valued identity, of objects and events, and of the moves that he is making to come out on top. It must be stressed, though, that the drama is not this real–life encounter, but a model of it. It uses the same 'linguistic mechanisms' in the same ephemeral setting, but it consciously serves a social end; it 'serves as a lifebelt to rescue us from an ocean of meaninglessness'.[10]

The game of drama then, as we can see, imitates the real–life inter–action of people. But every game has its 'payoff', that goal that makes it worth playing or worth watching. Most are obvious, the winning of the game by amassing points, beating the opponent, but what is the payoff in the drama game?

The aesthetic view

Susan Langer in *Feeling and Form* (26) offers what may be an answer to this question. The excitement, she would claim, results from our being given a highly selected abstract of life in such a simplified context that we are enabled to be predictive about its issues; we are able to foresee the futures of its characters, to apprehend a sense of destiny. Nor is this image of life, as in literature, presented in finished events, but in 'immediate, visible responses of human beings... Its basic abstraction is the act, which springs from the past, but is directed towards the future, and is always great with things to come'.[11]

This discernment is enjoyable for it contrasts with the real–life situation in which we are seldom able to predict with much certainty the outcome of our actions. Very often they are too numerous, too diffuse, for us to discern any overall pattern arising from them. But because the world of drama is the world of play and game, it observes the conditions of being, 'outside ordinary life'[12] and proceeding within 'its own proper boundaries of time and space according to fixed rules and in an orderly manner'. Therefore within this game of drama, as in any other, rules apply and among them the rule of irrelevance. This rule indicates what things shall or shall not be regarded as part of the action, what things shall command our attention and what may be ignored. This practise frame sharpens our focus on actions and their outcome; it raises our sense of expectancy yet preserves room for an enjoyable uncertainty. This is a concomitant of any game but perhaps most characteristic of drama, where 'this sense of destiny is paramount'.[13]

The Game in action

We have been arguing the case for looking at drama as a game, sometimes relating it to universally accepted games, and using terminology perhaps more at home with physical education. Let us then use a concrete example from a piece of dramatic dialogue to illustrate how it is that we receive this apprehension of destiny. The lines are taken from *Othello*, a play that smoulders and smokes with the awful, inevitable passion that ultimately consumes the characters. Here Iago plants the seeds of jealousy in the mind of Othello by suggesting that his wife Desdemona is the mistress of Cassio, one of his officers. Desdemona has just left them and Othello looks after her with an overwhelming burst of love., At the euphoric moment Iago begins the corruption:[14]

OTHELLO Excellent wretch! Perdition catch my soul
But I do love thee! and when I love thee not
Chaos is come again.
IAGO My noble lord, —
OTHELLO What dost thou say, Iago?
IAGO Did Michael Cassio, when you wooed my lady,
Know of your love?
OTHELLO He did, from first to last: why dost thou ask?
IAGO But for the satisfaction of my thought;
No further harm.
OTHELLO Why of thy thought, Iago?
IAGO I did not think he had been acquainted with her.
OTHELLO O, yes; and went between us very oft.
IAGO Indeed?
OTHELLO Indeed? Ay, indeed; discern'st though aught in that?
Is he not honest:
IAGO   Honest, my lord?
OTHELLO Honest? Ay, honest.
IAGO My lord, for aught I know.
OTHELLO What dost thou think?
IAGO   Think, my lord?
OTHELLO Think, my lord? By heaven, he echoes me,
As if there were some monster in his thought
Too hideous to be shown. Thou dost mean something:
I heard thee say but now, thou lik'st not that,
When Cassio left my wife: what didst not like?
And when I told thee he was of my counsel
In my whole course of wooing, thou criedst 'Indeed?'

> And didst contract and purse thy brow together,
> As if thou then hadst shut up in thy brain
> Some horrible conceit: if thou dost love me
> Show me thy thought.

IAGO   My lord, you know I love you.

So we see the poison beginning to spread, partly fed in by these half suggestions of Iago and partly from Othello's own insistence that there is some basis for the innuendoes.

Watching the play we are aware of the game that Iago is playing and how the innocent responses of Desdemona unwittingly assist his fearful scheme. No wonder that a lady, it is reported, unable to bear the tension once shouted out in the theatre, 'Why don't you believe her? You great, black fool!' Her vision of what must result from the actions happening before her eyes, her apprehension of destiny, was so painful that she no longer could be contained by the game restrictions. Langer analyses the process with consummate skill. When talking of destiny she says,

'It is what makes the present action seem like an integral part of the future, howbeit that future has not unfolded yet. The reason is that on the stage, every thought expressed in conversation, every feeling betrayed by voice or look, is determined by the total action of which it is a part – perhaps an embryonic part, the first hint of the motive that will soon gather force. Even before one has any idea of what the conflict is to be... one feels the tension developing. This tension between past and future, the theatrical 'present moment', is what gives to acts, situations, and even such constituent elements as gestures and attitudes and tones, the peculiar intensity known as 'dramatic quality'.[15]

For many of us, textual analysis is our most familiar experience of dramatic dialogue. But we must be wary of assuming that the form of the drama is contained merely in the written word. We will remember how Langer talked of 'immediate, visible responses', these actions that before our eyes assume the characteristic of form. Charles Williams calls the process 'form in suspense'[16] and holds it to be the essential dramatic illusion. He would insist that only when the play has been completed in performance is its form in existence. Furthermore, he suggests that the form the play takes is less important than 'that while the drama moves a form is being fulfilled'.[17] This momentum marries well with the earlier remarks we noted concerning the apprehension of destiny, and the question of order and meaning in the lives of men. Langer herself says that destiny does not exist as fact, but resembles 'an aspect of real experience, and, indeed a fundamental one, which distinguishes human life from animal existence: the sense of past and future as parts of one continuum, and therefore of life as a single reality.[18] Perhaps this is the way that drama serves as 'a lifebelt'.

The Drama Game

We have established, then, that drama is a game, what sort of game it is and how it works. But the definition is as yet diffuse because to support its validity we have drawn from a wide range of evidence. We are ready now to attempt a definition of our own of the dramatic process within the contextual framework of the game. But lest it appears strange and forbidding, let us first take the familiar game of cricket and present it in the same way, so we may see that something so well known in our experience can reappear in a sharp focus by redefinition.

Cricket is an open-air game played with a ball, bat and wickets between two sides of eleven players each. The duration of the game is limited and within that time each team attempts to win by amassing the highest number of runs, ie points, while preventing the opposition from scoring. The tactics employed to achieve success are many and varied and no two games of cricket are alike, except in their rules which define the aim of the game and the constraints within which that aim can be realised.

When we stand back like this, it is easier to discern which features are essential, and which are peripheral. For there is a danger that such things as the rituals that attend the more sophisticated games of cricket can obscure our remembrance that basically it is the same game as we may find in the backyard or on some Caribbean beach. There is an equal danger that we mistake the dead, institutionalised aspects of theatre practice for drama. A similar analysis as that which we have made of cricket, disregarding inessentials, may be equally valuable to our understanding of the dramatic process.

The most important feature of the drama is that it is a co-operative and not a competitive game. The players combine to present an imitation of social life, a fiction in which they pretend to be someone other than themselves. The verbal and non-verbal skills they employ realise that imitation in a set of encounters between the fictitious characters. It is not a story that is animated but a number of significant meetings that reflect upon what has gone before and what is yet to come. The creation of this sense of a living present, heavy with an impending future, is the aim of the players. It is not to convince that what is happening is real, but that what is happening is significant because the future is consequent upon it. And it is

21

only the drama that has the means to create such an immediate and compelling sense of present acts and future consequences: destiny, not as a literacy device, but as an awesomely visible outcome of people's interaction.

More succinctly we may express it thus: drama is a game in which the players, in role, present an analogy of social behaviour. They employ verbal and non-verbal skills in a series of encounters which, cumulatively, reveal the form of the analogy. The players do not aim at a convincing imitation of reality, but at the illusion of impending outcomes from immediate actions. The operation of this sense of destiny is the particular province of the drama game.

In the definition of both the games mentioned we may detect common elements; the operation of individual skills and the unity of group purpose. In the drama game, as perhaps in any game, the skills are exercised within the sanction of the group's agreement to play that game. This is because the game is essentially a social experience, and the drama, relying as it does upon 'the willing suspension of disbelief', is perhaps the most social of games. And though we may talk of the individual and his development through drama, we have to bear in mind that the social context of the experience will affect the freedom of that individuality.

Creativity: individual and group

It is in this very area of personal development and self-expression that we encounter the most colourful vagaries in drama manuals. Perhaps it is because what drama teachers do in their lessons, as Witkin repeatedly suggests in *The Intelligence of Feeling* (51), 'does not comprehend the creative process and remains external to the expressive act'.[19] This weakness springs partly from an inability to distinguish between reactive and reflective behaviour; between an impulse that results in behaviour that merely expresses disturbance, and one which results in behaviour that recalls the disturbance, thereby assimilating it. This leads to a 'knowing', ie 'an intermediate stage of acting in the head prior to acting in the world'.[20]

Encountering expressive acts, the teacher perceives only that all release sensate impulses, and in the absence of an ability to distinguish the creative, he justifies their existence in the lesson by deeming them 'cathartic', a means of 'discharging tensions, for getting one's feelings into some sort of external form'. And these sensate impulses that result in a whole 'disparate range of activities'[21] are mistakenly regarded as being subsumed under the tortured name of 'Drama'.

Witkin rightly insists that personal development must be the prime aim of progressive mastery of new and complex levels of sensate experience'.[22]

First one must come to respond to sensate problems and then to use one's response to recall the sensate disturbance, thereby resolving the problem that it sets.

A part of this mastery is a result of the ability to use an expressive form that is shaped by one's own 'reflexive control'. In other words to work in a medium the form of which is a suspended one, as we mentioned earlier. In drama, certainly, form is created in the moment-to-moment exchange, not from the animation of a set of instructions. We must accept that the 'feeling form' we recognise as drama, however, emerges from the individual but in concert with others. Also we cannot ignore that the players maintain a role; their sensate impulse is projected into expression that appears as the behaviour of someone other than their true selves. And the continued existence of these insubstantial characters depends upon the veracity of their interaction, a veracity dependent upon sincere sensate impulse and on a common fund of experience from which the reflective behaviour is derived. This communion is essential to drama, and its neglect, which can be encouraged by too great an emphasis on 'the individuality of individuals', can confound our understanding of the workings of the dramatic process.

Glynne Wickham put his finger on this danger when in the DES publication *Trends* in 1968 he reviewed the recently published 'Education Survey 2: Drama' (54). In his concluding paragraph he wrote:

'Drama as therapy, drama as history, drama as literature, drama as recreation or drama as physical education are all useful and interesting by-products of the subject; but if drama is not recognised as first and last an art form and taught in that context, all the efforts which have been made and are being made to re-establish it as a subject within the whole age group spectrum of education today... will degenerate into a posse of rival factions destined in their determination to outbid each other, to effect the total dismissal of the drama from all classrooms for years to come.'

His warning has proved true in so far as there is as much confusion today about what constitutes drama and what our aims are when using it in schools. Teachers still quarrel about approaches – movement, text, mime, etc, without any real understanding of the essential dramatic process. It is as though there were endless discussion about the best way to kick a football without any agreement about why the game requires you to kick a football at all. The controversy is further complicated by a body of opinion that doubts whether there is any value in having the drama game in schools at all. Supporters of this view are sceptical of the catharsis argument and see only a reactive behaviour that resembles what normally is to be seen in the school playground. And in the absence of evidence that the child is developing the mastery of sensate experience mentioned earlier, who is to blame them?

Nevertheless perhaps because drama teachers have had to work in this climate of disbelief, if not downright hostility, they are acutely aware of their dilemma of releasing in their lessons what is illegitimate expression. For if the child is working from impulse then the individuality of his response may penetrate the fabric of the school's norms and values. We need consider nothing more complicated than the incidence of noise through group talking.

Language

Silence in many schools is naturally still regarded as a virtue for it constitutes to a large degree the ideal atmosphere for instruction. In view of this and because they have encountered the futility of attempting to change such an attitude, where it exists, many drama teachers have devised activities, which they would call dramatic, that bypass the necessity for speech. Mime, dance and dance drama have replaced the genuinely dramatic experience at the heart of which must be language, one of the essential factors in our daily social life of which drama is a model.

The language of words and of movement is an important feature of the feeling form because it represents a growing capacity for organisation, 'a vital faculty which allows particular areas of reality to be described and communicated.'[23] What should be remembered though is the point made earlier that the great realm of verbal and non-verbal interchange is the world in which we all daily operate. Children acquire these skills at a very early age, using language in encounters with immense subtlety and understanding. And if what they wish to express is clear and acceptable to them they do not need elaborate warm-up exercises nor artificial aids to concentration to motivate speech.

Not only do children have a fund of language resources which the teacher can draw upon, but also they have already had considerable experience in using language dramatically. Unconsciously children develop dramatic skills in early childhood, skills that serve essentially the same purpose as the now largely estranged art of drama. Indeed the dramatic process serves as a continuum through life differing only in the degree of constraints that attend it. Our ability to handle the form with purpose yet maintaining its spontaneity, in fact being free within the constraints, marks our progress towards preserving an equilibrium in life. And yet to be able to do this depends not upon a discursive study of the form but upon our continuing to respond with feeling to life around us and within us.

We have dwelt upon the nature of Drama using the Game analogy to establish what we mean when we use the term. The references have been frequently applied to the teaching context rather than to the theatre and by implication there have been certain assumptions about the nature of Education. Perhaps before we apply our understanding of the subject further, we should spend a little more time on an examination of what sorts of experience contribute to one's learning and in what ways drama relates to them. From such a foundation we might then proceed to examine the child's experience at various stages and finally the adult contact with theatre and how it remains as a formative educational influence.

Summary

This chapter argues that the confusion surrounding drama teaching springs not only from misunderstood methodology but from a basic ignorance of the nature of the dramatic process. To assist an understanding of the concept, and as an analytic tool for evaluating the teaching of drama, the Game is introduced as a more familiar, yet synonymous, experience. The association is shown to be supported linguistically, historically and aesthetically, and from this theoretical basis a working definition of the drama is presented to be used within the various contexts described in the subsequent chapters.

Notes

1   Huizinga (22) page 32
2   Way (47) page 7
3   Goodridge (13) page 1
4   Kolve (25) page 20
5   Kolve (25) page 15
6   Kolve (25) page 20
7   Lymann and Scott (28) page 9
8   Lymann and Scott (28) page 8
9   Lymann and Scott (28) page 10
10 Bentley (3) page 147
11 Langer (26) page 306
12 Huizinga (22), page 32
13 Langer (26) page 308
14 Shakespeare (40) page 64
15 Langer (26) page 308
16 Hands (56) page 61-7
17 Hands (56) pages 61-7
18 Langer (26) pages 311
19 Witkin (51) page 35
20 Witkin (51) page 9
21 Witkin (51) page 34
22 Witkin (51) page 49
23 Williams (50) page 34
24 Britton (4) page 117

Further Reading

With the exception of Williams (50), Witkin (51) and Langer (26) all the books recommended here are concerned partly with the concept of Game.

Huizinga's wide-ranging survey of human play activity (22) taps anthropology and etymology for its material as well as more traditional historical sources.

Kolve (25) and Wickham (49) both demonstrate the indivisibility of Game and Drama in the Middle Ages, linking the model with the social conventions and beliefs of its time.

Goffman (12) introduces the Game/actor analysis of social life in his very readable book. In (11) he extends the idea into a study of interaction. In that it relates to simulated relationships between characters and the actual actor/audience relationships, its relevance to drama is inescapable.

As the Game concept helps one recognise the constraints of the dramatic process, Langer and Witkin maintain the balance that reminds us of its aetheticism. Both are concerned with the creative act, including the recipient. William (50) returns us to the social necessity of art.

2

Education and the Classroom

Life in Classrooms
Perhaps because we have all experienced living in classrooms we do not look at the social aspects but only the instructional. Even teachers who encounter classroom conditions every day do not regard them as extraordinary but see only the peripheral characteristics. These exterior things exist as a result of the teacher-directed classroom organisation and control but do not penetrate the heart of the social structures and relationships. These Jackson identifies as appearing in three major ways – 'as members of crowds, as potential recipients of praise or reproof, and as pawns of institutional authorities.' In these ways 'students are confronted with aspects of reality that at least during their childhood years are relatively confined to the hours spent in classrooms.' And whatever else may be learned during those long hours, it seems likely, Jackson continues, 'adaptive strategies having relevance for other contexts and other life periods are developed.'[1]

'Crowds, praise and power' make the environment in which learning takes place and are themselves a major part of what is learned. They represent areas of social control to which we learn to respond and comply, and in the process we lose our individuality and the significance of individual experience. Especially is this true of being part of a crowd where 'delay, denial, interruption and social distraction' prevent not only one's own desires being fulfilled but also an effective contribution to the fulfilment of those of others. These frustrations produce not a productive anger but an all-pervasive lethargy, the celebrated apathy about which organisers wring their hands. We learn to live in schools with unutterable boredom brought about by time unsatisfactorily handled and through the death of desire.

Neither the praise nor the anger of the teacher ultimately can do very much to change the attitudes that living as a crowd induces. Children, especially at secondary school level, give up trying because praise becomes

27

to be seen not as a reward for genuine effort but as a veiled exhortation always to do better. Evaluation by the teacher or by peers in classrooms so often represents a process external to the child's influence. Rarely is he consulted about his own estimation of his progress nor indeed what for him represents progress. A child-centered approach is a rarity, for the norm reflects training that stresses the need for the teacher to be always in control of everything that happens in the classroom. Surely there can be few situations in which a crowd of people is expected to comply so consistently with the orders of one individual.

Like the apathy we so often deplore in our society, the roots of an unquestioning acceptance of authority in adult life may very well begin in the classroom. Rules become restrictions because they do not represent a genuine contract but a situation in which there are oppressors and oppressed. Yet such is the ease and the security of the adaptive strategies that the occurrence of the unusual or the challenge of the innovative to the individual initiative is met with resentment and anger. Approaches in the classroom, therefore, that depart from the traditional, will often spell disaster as we shall see when we consider how the experience of drama threatens dead, institutionalised attitudes by stirring the essential individuality of the class members.

Before the claims for the effects of drama in the classroom appear to become incredibly excessive, let us return to the Game association to underpin the assertions. In particular let us examine those same characteristics – crowds, praise and power – in relation to the Drama Game and see whether they pose the same problems.

Rules

Central to the examination is the question of authority and rule-regulation in particular. 'Obedience to rules is a freely given act of the will among equals... In obedience to rules we reserve the right to question and criticise, but since the will of equals is the basis for the authority of rules, differences must be resolved through arbitration.'[2] If we apply this statement to the conduct of any game, we know it to be true for the progress of the game, as indeed its very existence, depends on the desire to play for the satisfaction gained therefrom. Heavy authoritarian control of games, as again we remember from schooldays, can destroy for ever our desire to participate. And it is even more applicable to the Drama Game where the content is so dependent upon a corporate act of willing suspension of disbelief. Authority then is vested in each member of the class through a self-restraint exercised in order to achieve the desired goal. Such power sharing does not eliminate the need for the teacher, but his role is clearly that of facilitator and not policeman.

Evaluation

Equally it may be the function of the teacher to be arbiter but not the sole judge of the work of the children. The criteria for the evaluation of what is achieved by the class, either collectively or individually, must arise from the nature of the task. Once the class is clear about what it wants to do then it will be equally clear about whether it has succeeded in its aim. Especially in the arts where the affective is paramount there comes a satisfaction from creative expression that is unmistakable. In terms of skills of performance as Brecht says, 'If it works, it works'. The same may be said of the content or the form of the piece, for both may have their own inbuilt logic. For the teacher therefore to criticise using alien criteria for assessment is to be merely irrelevant. He must instead be able to come to terms with what is being created, to enter the child's world and obey its logic, as indeed in the theatre we submit ourselves to the circumstances and characters with which we are presented. And by so penetrating the fantasy the teacher is able to provoke the child's thought, but always contextually. As Joan Tough has said, 'the teacher is projecting into what is meaningful for the child, knowing his background and using that, reporting upon what has happened to him outside, making his own past experience important to her as a teacher'. (53) What is wrong is when the teacher praises or blames children either because he assumes his job is to hand down judgements or because he believes that his own experience is definitive.

Delay

Finally in this part of the argument, it would be ridiculous to assert that drama in the classroom is not subject to the same frustrations of 'delay, denial, interruption and social distraction'. Indeed, because the basis of the work is consensual, all these factors may be even more apparent. There is however a difference in that there is a positive fervour to overcome the obstructions in order to reach one's goal. A parallel may be seen in Play and Game of any sort where a number of people is involved. Their desire to play enables them to accept interruptions, to settle differences along the way and to recognise that the pace of the game must accommodate the slowest player. It is truly a shared experience and to a certain degree the solving of the problems of distractions is part of the strength of the overall success of the group. Clearly there is a limit to the extent to which the momentum of the play can be interrupted for it can kill the desire to play altogether. Here is a good lesson for the teacher who feels the need constantly to stop the progress of what is happening in order to gain what he considers clarification. Like football players shivering on the field waiting for the recommencement of play, drama players too may feel their inspiration dissipating while details of plot or character are being exhaustively analysed by the teacher.

The watchword that applies throughout is 'sharing'; shared motivation, shared experience, shared responsibility and shared success. Living in crowds, which happens both in and out of school, does not pose a threat to individuality if the life of a community is one of shared experience. Problem solving and decision making needs to involve the talents of us all, tolerance and respect for others grows from an assurance that they are extended to oneself. Rewards and privileges, if they have a place at all, should emerge from a genuine communal acclaim.

These are all social experiences that we would claim are possible where the mode of government is democratic. We extol the values that they represent and often act as though the society in which we live practised them. Yet this is patently not the case and so it seems that the education of the young prepares them to accept the lie with equanimity. They are not taught to question the obvious and obscene discrepancy between life as it is claimed to be and as it actually is for many millions of people. It would be easy to pillory the Press, politicians, the media and other social institutions for these double standards, but we are all guilty, for we are all so compliant. But, as we said earlier, it may be that part of that unquestioning acquiescence begins in the classroom.

Education should assist the appreciation and conservation of socially healthy and beneficial norms and values but it should do this by encouraging question and debate. We should know what we believe in and why, for without that conviction our worthwhile social institutions will be destroyed. Yet it remains that in our classrooms we conduct activities that do not encourage children to question, to debate, to evaluate, to live together as socially healthy and responsible people, to help to fashion the world of which they are its most optimistic part. Our hope for a better future must be the result of our confidence in the young for they must achieve what we have failed to do. And unless we offer them the means through education, we have only ourselves to blame.

Drama: the democratic model

Ideally drama serves as a truly democratic model, for it is above all else consensual. It both celebrates social values and challenges them, thereby assisting the process of social change, so necessary to the health of a community. This has been its social function since its origins, a function that has been increasingly neglected as industrialism has destroyed community life and community consciousness. But the roots remain and the Drama represents one of the ways in which they can be nourished. This is particularly apparent in Community Arts developments where people will use Drama to explore and express their perceptions of a social issue. This is the genuine educative use of the Drama and yet it is not yet widespread in our schools. The reasons are perhaps those that we have examined, that the school system as we know it is not conducive to the democratic relationships that are essential for the conduct of the work. This observation will not be welcomed by many who would consider that they conduct drama in school, by the writers of drama manuals or by the producers of work cards or other materials for use in the classroom. They would point to the progress that has been made to make drama an acceptable part of the curriculum, its coverage in Bullock and the things that are written and said about it by Inspectors and in the Schools Council. What we see around us, however, is not the reflection of today's attitudes but those of the last decade which have been realised in buildings, staff and other resources. To see the results of present thinking we shall have to wait for a while. There are nevertheless sufficient indications upon which to make some predictions and some of these were referred to in the opening paragraph of chapter 1. And even were we to look back to the sixties as a supportive time for drama nevertheless what was prescribed was a long way from the experience described earlier.

Nowhere is this clearer than in many of the manuals where the lesson plans are teacher-centred, authoritarian models posing as open-ended lessons. One such manual says explicitly that it contains what should be done but not how to do it, while others offer a host of ideas for the teacher unable to conceive his own and too insecure to invite others from the class. Above all the models do not attempt to change a school environment of authoritarianism but accommodate it by advocating activities that deny the pupil freedom of choice, freedom of speech and even freedom of movement. And increasingly we have moved nearer to an acceptable drama image, one that is indistinguishable from other lessons in which the emphasis is on conformity to externally set standards through prescribed curriculum.

'Arts and the Adolescent' and Witkin's, 'The Intelligence of Feeling' have stressed the necessity for an area of genuine creativity in the Creative Arts. Too often, though, teachers provide not only the stimulus but also, by a variety of means, determine the response of the class. The DES report, 'Education Survey 2: Drama' back in 1968 despairingly looked for the children's contribution in much of the work they saw. Nor should we comfort ourselves by saying that things have changed, for recent films showing drama teachers at work reveal the same imposition, though the accompanying notes suggest that the teacher's view of what he is doing is the exact opposite. Unconsciously teachers mould the work to fit the prevailing school situation which is one in which the teacher has the ideas and the pupils have none.

Certainly a notable exception to this pessimistic view of drama teaching is that work that has been developed in the North East of England. Dorothy Heathcote and Gavin Bolton have explored the area of provocation in drama teaching. They are the spike in the side of a class urging them on to make their own choice of play and then to follow through the implications of their choice in role playing. Further they have concentrated upon the analysis of the teacher/class interaction in the drama lesson. They identify clearly what the role of the drama is in the learning situation and in what ways the teacher can assist, allowing the play to remain child-centred. Their approach rarely calls into question the admissibility of drama in the school context largely because their approach is essentially contract learning. The contract is established through a series of questions, the answers to which commit a class to a course of action. Throughout there are reminders of their original intention which can be changed but only as a conscious decision backed by reasonable argument. In this way the class is caused to reflect upon the cause and effect of human actions, how they confirm or deny social values and how they affect others for better or worse.

Working in this way requires not only that the teacher should be aware of in what ways the question can further the progress of the work by provoking thought and feeling, but also when is the most effective time to do so. This is the intuitive area of teaching that requires the teacher to penetrate the conscious level of the thinking of the class and to feel for the developmental possibilities of what is yet half formed. Above all the teacher must be clear about the direction in which the work is heading and where it now stands. Without such insight the play becomes too diffuse; the blind lead the blind. So it is crucial that the teacher has access to some means of analysis, some map that is sufficiently familiar in its appearance that he can learn where he and the class have got lost.

Such a guide can be found in the consideration of Drama as Game, for experience of games is something with which we are all very familiar. And though skills and strategies are learned, it requires an intuitive grasp of what is happening to enable players to apply them effectively in the dynamic of play. At any time, however, in the progress of the game it is possible to stop and take stock, whether it be to sort out a problem, review a piece of play that has taken place, or plan the strategy of the moves ahead. All of this is possible in the Drama game which can help the teacher and the class to enjoy playmaking through effective planning and operation.

The chapters that follow examine the characteristics of the Drama Game in various circumstances. And, in that the study follows the chronological development of children in schools to their adult experience in the community, it is hoped it will reveal the process of drama as a constant in the changing picture of the constraints that attend it.

We begin with a look at the way the young child acquires and manipulates skills that are recognisably dramatic. Especially important to the process is the adults' acceptance and encouragement of the play activity. And although parents and teachers do not always recognise this intense learning process, without active discouragement the child supplies his own structures within which he experiments.

Although it may seem fanciful at this stage, it is hoped it will be shown that the child operates the dramatic process within his make-believe play to those same ends that we have introduced, namely, to preserve our view of the world from fragmentation and disharmony, to maintain it as something we can continue to live with as happily as may be.

Summary
This chapter examines the relationship between Jackson's analysis of life in classrooms with its attendant constraints of 'delay, denial, interruption and social distraction', and the Drama as a model of the democratic process. It is suggested that ends of Education, rarely realised in social terms, are more recognisable in the child-centred experience of Drama, a consensually maintained task regulated by social contract.

Notes
[1] Jackson (23) page 11   [2] Duncan (60) page 326

Further Reading
Jackson looks coldly at the repressive processes of our schools which contrasts with Duncan's ideal view of the social process. Witkin and Ross find support for Jackson in their survey. Bolton and Wagner on Heathcote present a careful study of teacher/pupil relationships maintained and enhanced by drama. Their work reflects more the concept of contract learning.

3

Drama and the Young Child

The aim of this chapter is to examine how the young child, in his make-believe play, recreates and represents experience. We shall see how this is achieved through using his own voice and body as a symbol for phenomena that do not actually exist. Also, most important, we shall recognise how in role he uses language as anticipatory commentary; as a plan of future consequences arising from present action in which he is engaged. Lastly we shall relate his natural ability to be both participant and spectator at the same time to widen social implications and especially the appreciation of the art of drama.

For the young person, learning is literally 'child's play'. Adults use the phrase contemptuously for indicating what is easy and inconsequential; a puritanical view perhaps of enjoyable sensate experience. Certainly fun is the principal motivating factor in all Play and Game and is the enviable aspect of children's pastimes that we both observe and remember from our own childhood.

Make-believe play and drama
Less obvious, though well appreciated by educationists, are the derivatives of that play, for not only does the child benefit physically but also in his cognitive and affective growth. Of especial interest here is the make-believe play of young children, for this resembles most closely the drama as defined earlier.

Nevertheless commentators differ in how they interpret the distinction. Some will insist on a complete separation especially if they plead the cause of child drama as an autonomous form. Others are more inclined to distinguish between spontaneous dramatic play and the use of the child's ability to imitate and employ mimicry to animate narrative.

This latter activity is a familiar feature of the infant classroom for its structure provides a secure framework for the teacher. Equally familiar is the theatre from that supports Nativity Plays and those representations that appear in end of term concerts. The main feature of them is directed speech and movement with costumes and other more or less elaborate theatrical constraints.

For the supporters of both schools, the structured and the unstructured there are misgivings; for the latter group to harness the energy and direct it towards perceived educational goals easily leads to the imposition of adult concepts. For the other group it is disturbingly evident how different is the response of children to teacher-directed work from the vigour and energy of child-centred creative activity. Perhaps both views start from the wrong end in not appreciating the Play and Game element in the adult drama form. Too often teaching manuals represent Drama experience through life as separate, stratified layers with their own unique characteristics. Rather we should regard the drama as a rich vein that has the same essential characteristics wherever one taps to find it. The child's experience is not therefore uniquely different but simply less elaborate with an emphasis upon the exploratory rather than the communicative aspects of the dramatic process.

The child still largely egocentric in his view of society does not make the conscious dramatic statement that was identified earlier in the definition of drama. He does, however, create the same illusion of the significant present but without the adult's sense of its symbolic application. Both forms are heavily structured although the dramatic play of young children is often referred to as being 'unencumbered by structure'[1] or 'Free Play'.[2]

Confusion arises when one assumes that there is no shape, no plan that regulates play activity. As we found in Huizinga's definition in the first chapter, although play is 'a free activity'[3] it nevertheless 'proceeds within its own proper boundaries of time and space according to fixed rules and in an orderly manner'.[4] Now with the young child's play, that regulation arises from his own initiative and, because play is often solitary, is not subject to group agreement. But it does not lack regulation, for though it may be brief and transitory, the rules are there, though, as adults, we may not recognise their embryonic appearance.

Language as regulator

The overriding regulator of dramatic or symbolic play is language. This is not to deny that in this activity the child's movement is a major expressive component. Nor must it be thought that the child's use of language resembles those patterns of dialogue that we are used to in the adult form. Talk in this representation, as with 'all other forms of representation that play their part in behaviour', as Britton points out in *Language and Learning*

(4) 'plays an organising role'.[5] Indeed, citing the work of the Russian psychologist, Luria, as evidence of the regulatory role of language, Britton suggests that in this capacity it is essential to make-believe play.

For somewhere about the age of three the child's use of speech undergoes a significant and very important change. His 'ability both to understand and to use words comes to rely less and less on the cues offered by the present situation: that is to say, words begin to stand in place of things'.(6) Thus whereas earlier he would be unable to handle in speech ideas of a past or future except in relation to things immediately present, later he can recall and predict without having to require the present reality of objects, people, events, etc.

Participant and spectator

James Britton, whose work is referred to often in this chapter, makes a distinction between the way we use language in our everyday experience. The first is when we use language in response to ongoing events, the participant form; the second, the spectator form arises not from the immediate, but in recollection or in premeditation of events. The former speech is used to organise our behaviour, to regulate both our individual and our co-operative activities. Britton further suggests that by such use of language, its participants are able to construct a representation of experience and continue to adjust it; to take it in their stride as they encounter the unexpected. In the spectator form, however, 'language is used to refer to, report upon, and interpret action, rather than in substitution for it'.[10] This speech form enables us to shape our experience and to share with others whose reception verifies our understanding; 'Human community grows by the discovery of common meanings and common means of communication'.[11] Also we are able to speculate upon future events, to muse upon the 'might-be'.

The role of the participant, then, may be seen as one in which decision-making and action are paramount characteristics. For the spectator, unburdened with the responsibility for immediate response to a situation, comes the freedom to 'evaluate more broadly, to savour feelings, and to contemplate *forms* – the formal arrangement of feelings, of events... of ideas, and the forms of the language, spoken or written, in which the whole is expressed'.[12] And from both aspects of experience, especially the second, we are better able to arrive at an understanding of who and what we are.

Rightly it is asserted that dramatic or make-believe play is performing a spectator role; it is the organising of past experience in a recreated world, not dealing with the real world at first hand. Susanna Millar puts paradox of play well when she calls it, 'exploring what is familiar, practising what has already been mastered, friendly aggression, sex without coition, excitement about nothing....'[13] And it is in this paradoxical situation that we find participant and spectator at one and the same time.

We have said earlier that drama creates a world within a world and that the created world is seriously treated. Peter Slade in *Child Drama* (43) identifies this prerequisite in his terms 'absorption and sincerity',[14] without which drama is impossible. This agreement to suspend disbelief and to abide by the often illogical conditions of the created world is as central to every other game as it is to drama. The rugby football player must advance by throwing the ball behind him; the boxer must not continue to punch his opponent after the bell has rung, even though he may be in sight of victory; if you land on one of my hotels in 'Monopoly' you pay, even if it breaks you.

In drama, though, not only do we create the world but also the people that inhabit that world. For the players in the game of drama employ their communication skills in role; they are putting themselves into the shoes of someone else and their speech becomes correspondingly appropriate. It should be noted, though that the appropriateness is in no way confined to oddities of character. It is not only that the players develop mere idiosyncrasies, a 'funny' voice, but that their speech accords with the demands of the created world. In fact their speech, as characters, reflects their need to make decisions, to act in the face of a challenging situation; their role is a participant one in the press of the created reality.

The relationships of these fictional people are always seen in the context of stress. Essentially in drama there is conflict, a problem requiring resolution or alleviation in a social context where decisions must affect others for better or worse. The urgency that the crisis imposes heightens the critical importance of the decisions being made from moment to moment, and reveals to the observer the presence of the working of 'destiny'.

The creation of this other world is the conscious choice of the player, either alone or in concert with others if the game is for more than one. The setting, characters, events, all arise as a reworking of past experience or as a projection into future possibilities. The role of the players is a spectator role, even as they, themselves, experience the stress of their created world. There is a high degree of selection, of shaping by the players as the action proceeds, for they are 'not really *being* so-and-so, but *representing* such-and-such'.[15] We will again recall Huizinga's comments on the function of play when he suggested it was the representation of a contest.

With the play of young children, where the constraints exercised by the spectator role are overt and explicit, we see the players absorbed in the action as characters, but accompanying the action with a stream of commentary that is regulatory instruction. This example from a group of five-year-old boys illustrates the process at work:

Three boys have come into the play corner aware of what they are going to play. *A* has assigned *B* the role of a robber.

B I do' like being robbers.
C Let me go. I am a robber.
B *Don't* want to be a robber.
A *(Indicating C)* Neil is going to be the robber.
B Yes, you can be the robber.
A All right, go over there. *(C goes out).*
A *(Sings and dials number on toy telephone...* Who is it... Police?... please come... catch the robbers. *(Puts down 'phone)*
A *(to B)* Come on, put that down, come over here. *(Looks out of play-house window)* It's not going to rain. You phone them.
B But... I think I'd better call. *(Goes to telephone, dials, mutters, puts phone down)* Coming now. *(Crosses to A)* Coming right away.
A Good... I'm glad they are.

During the time of observation the boys, who left the play corner after this conversation, did not appear to continue the 'robber' game. C did not rejoin them and A and B both played on the slide.

Though the dramatic episode is very brief it has all the elements we have discussed. First it is a game with the allotment of functions to the players. The structure is maintained by the regulating comments, especially those of A who dominates the play. He, in role, establishes the tension of the piece by his terse, whispered telephone conversation. When he employs B in the more relaxed atmosphere of, 'It's not going to rain', he asks him to perform something *he has already done himself.* But the use of 'phone *them'* makes it more than a mere instruction to use the telephone. B imitates A's action but introduces a new element in the urgent present, that the police are on their way. A responds to the new development, and the play which might be called 'Getting the Police', is finished with the obvious relief of 'I'm glad they are'.

The play, which apparently satisfied the players, is not animation of a plot, but, like all drama, is its exploration in the context of the significant present. Equally, children do not play 'mothers and fathers', but an encounter concerning these characters, in a present charged with possible future implications. And if we regard drama as a continuum, we shall see that to experience *Hamlet* in performance is to encounter the presence of 'destiny' in the same way, not to see the dramatisation of Lamb's *Tales from Shakespeare.*

Very often the speech that children use to accompany their play appears as planning speech only – 'Now mummy's going out'. 'The rain's stopped so we can go', 'Now *eat* dinner, come on', 'Eat dinner, lovely big spiders... cut them up'. Though it precipitates action it does so as participant speech, for the child is playing 'Mummy' when it is uttered. And, of course, so often in families, when adults use their role titles in talking to children, they use a sort of third person – 'Mummy will be cross', 'Daddy's tired, he can't come now', 'Mummy's going out'. In the home of the young child the adult uses language in this regulatory way constantly to define the situation of the child. Maybe that definition is to promote action, to persuade the child to comply with adult wishes. Certainly, very often the situations are ones that can create tensions for both adults and children, and it is this tension that is being represented in play and being come to terms with.

Though this therapeutic function of dramatic play is important, we must not lose sight of its role in the child's cognitive development. Both Piaget and Vigotsky consider such play, especially with its stream of commentary, as overt thinking. This process becomes interiorised as the child grows, and becomes unvoiced thought.

The DES *Education Survey 2: Drama,* suggests that the desire to play dramatically does not diminish as the child grows older. Certainly from classes that are family-grouped it is obvious that children at the upper end of the age range use the play corner as frequently if the opportunity is provided. This is particularly so when the corner is not 'excessively domestic', but 'includes blocks, rostra, packing cases and clothes and materials for dressing up, as well as an almost endless variety of other oddments'. Space for such play 'is needed in classrooms, in corridors, on the verandah, in all kinds of places inside and outside school'.[16] Then we may find that the play reflects the variety of experiences the child has to recreate as part of his conceptual thinking. The need for such expressive freedom is highlighted by Susanna Millar when she writes, 'If it is correct to describe make-believe play as thinking in action with few constraints, it is almost a truism that its content is dictated by whatever is of current interest to the child. Whatever is new, impressive, connected with something important in his life, or part of a rule or recurring pattern, or otherwise emphasised, is likely to have some priority of being selected'.[17]

The child's fund of such experiences will be enriched by the teacher who is able 'to come to terms with what they are doing'.[18] Then assuming this to be possible, how does the teacher extend and enrich what appears to be essentially a child-centred creation? This is a most crucial question for it affects all drama that might follow.

The report quoted earlier suggests that the child's play 'will be enriched by such resources as they may acquire in movement, in language, in sound and music, by their familiarity with poetry and narrative literature'. However, lest this might appear largely a question of teacher input, it is stressed that 'teachers should take every opportunity to get children used to putting ideas, thoughts, feelings, and observations into words'.[19] Clearly here is the dilemma; how far can one take the provision of stimulating material without allowing it to become so pervasive that it inhibits original work?

Drama and Story

Many drama manuals for teachers will suggest story as a starting point for dramatic work. Especially with young children the framework of the narrative would seem to assist the shaping of play that is 'endless, timeless, shapeless and unselective'. We should be wary, however, of giving unqualified support to this assumption, for it may be its substitution for the dramatic experience may be disastrous. The Drama Report examines briefly the distinction between 'dramatising known stories and encouraging children to make up their own plays'. It asks whether the constraints of 'the precise form that is laid down by the original chain of events' may not be too difficult for children to relate to their own invention. Strongly it asserts that, 'The belief expressed from time to time that children come closer to a story by acting it than simply listening to it is not always borne out in practice'.[20]

We should always be on our guard as adults that we do not unconsciously satisfy our own needs for security, when we favour the tidier structure of the linear plot. It may well be that many teachers are unaware that drama is not primarily a story, like a novel, but is a complexive blueprint that does not seek to cover a wide range of human experiences, but seeks to penetrate a small area deeply. Too often we equate the progress of the class with mere progression through a set of procedures. It can happen that the teacher supplies all the thought and the class the action. Unhappily this applies especially to the work of young children, and to their drama in particular.

The Drama Report suggests 'that children like to create a situation in which they are at home, and which they enjoy, and then to remain in it. Rapid and disconnected action is not a common feature of children's improvised drama and is often a sign of emotional immaturity'.[21] Bearing this in mind, one wonders what is the value of this:

41

'One morning you are fast asleep in bed; the alarm clock rings, so you push back the blankets and the sheets, put on your slippers and go to the bathroom; then you wash your face and hands – and don't forget your neck and behind your ears; and you clean your teeth...' and so on.[22] The work represents the build up of detail; 'discovering for themselves how to do each thing'. As the experience grows we enrich the experience by the type of suggestion that draws further detailed thinking and imagining from each person'.[23] Now though the author cautions against 'developing drama itself' so that we 'dash onwards to the next experience', his examples do just that. Wisely he says that much of the development of the 'story... can arise from discussion with the class, even during the actual running of the activity'.[24] Unfortunately, though, such examples often prove more attractive and more immediately acceptable, partly because they are so much safer for teachers; having children animate the teacher's monologue is so much easier to control than genuine creative thought and child invention.

The teacher who was able to come to terms with the following improvisation on the theme of the Nativity must have had a genuine feeling for the logic of children's drama:

'Another class in the same school had managed to work some diverting material of their own into the story of the Nativity. The boys disposed of the girls – the finding of parts for whom constitutes a perpetual problem – by making them sheep and driving them into a stockade which they had constructed out of chairs. Being shepherds they mounted guard and took advantage of the opportunity for a lengthy gossip. There was then another brilliant piece of invention. The shepherds were attacked by a wolf. Here there was justifiable opportunity for a fight of which they took full advantage. Finally, the wolf was killed and the shepherds applied themselves to digging a hole for burial. When the body of the wolf had been lowered in, the girls who had escaped being cast as sheep, appeared on the rostrum with great effect as Gabriel and the angels'.[25]

The experience clearly is not animated narrative but a set of encounters in which the resources of the shepherds are tested in a group situation. How unlike the following piece of dialogue for shepherds from a Nativity Play; The punctuation attempts to recreate the delivery of the lines:[26]

A Have-we-been-dreaming?

B The - angel - told - us - to - go - to - the - city - of - David.

C That — is — Bethlehem. LetusgotoBethlehemtoseethiswonder.

A What-about-our-sheep? We-should-not-leave-them.

B The-*angel*-told-us-to-go. *He*-will-guard-them.

This represents an extreme, though by no means uncommon, example of a teacher-dominated work for children. There are other forms more subtle, but equally constricting of invention and thought. Often what has a surface appearance of being spontaneous, original work is, in fact, the child's perception of the teacher's expectations clearly signalled in the choice of music, the way a question is posed, or in the reception of an answer, or suggestion. Reading the teacher's wishes is a skill that children learn quickly because it enables them to succeed or at least survive.

Questioning

The story, then, is valuable in that it provides a framework, but the stuff of drama is the exploration of the material within that framework. Here lies invention, imagination and originality encouraged by teachers aware of their employment of thinking skills techniques. 'Close questioning of the pupils by the teacher has led to deep involvement or a sense of relevance so that a new dimension has been added to apparently threadbare themes. 'All right, so you're on a desert island ... how did you get there? Who are you? Are you alone or with anyone?'[27] The questions are not intended to compose a story but to build up a sense of belief in the situation that is emerging. Interest grows from a sense of the dramatic potential and an increasing involvement with its concerns. To return to the game model, this is when it is being explored whether a game is possible and if so what sort of drama game. We shall return to this point later when we discuss the content and the conduct of the drama lesson. For now it is enough to stress that questioning skills are of paramount importance in assisting children's dramatic work at all ages. This is where the teacher can assist most in clarifying intention and yet avoid superimposition. The work of Barrett, Bloom or Guszak in outlining a taxonomy of comprehension skills, clearly can be adapted to the circumstances of the drama class. Such areas as remembering, organising, predicting and evaluating are vital to the successful definition of the area of inquiry that a group wishes to explore through drama. Such questioning does not necessarily precede or follow the dramatic work but takes place as the need for definition becames clear. And though it is true that we should 'not allow too much talking to take place before action begins,'[28] yet we should be aware that controlled discussion is providing experience that will be recoded and assimilated anew in the dramatic game. Too early release to action often produces only a superficial concern with plot and a busy moving on of the narrative.

Certainly 'with infants, the conflict needs to be of circumstance rather than character, since their main interest is in the action.'[29] But as the action is carried through the interaction of people in stress circumstances, the base of their invention must still be personal experience. For example, a class of 'top infants' on a hot June day had come in from the playground after dinner. Sticky and red they were cooling off in the shade of the school hall with its cold block floor. A boy asked whether he might have a drink of water and the teacher said no, because there was no water, it had all been used up. Though the class discovered that this was not so, in fact, the unexpected and unusual news made them look at the supply of domestic water in a new way. They discussed with the teacher what they knew of desert people and how such common commodities as water and salt were, for these people, almost luxuries. What sort of price would they put on water, asked the teacher, and with what would you want to be paid, money or goods. The idea of barter took the fancy of the class and soon the teacher had assisted the class to become an Arab village visited by a camel train desperate for water. The teacher's input was of the order of, 'How do you think they would...? Would they all...? What do you think the camelmen would have said about...?' Some questions preceded, some intervened: above all the teacher knew when to be quiet and let such would-be queries arise and be answered in the play itself. Suffice it to say that the haggling was the drama and that it ran a good twenty minutes. One girl at the end was delighted to have got 'some red material to make my husband a pair to trousers', but a camel driver was disgusted to have been asked 'for a copy of *The Times* or *The Guardian*'. The game of the water bargaining was played with great seriousness, the situation was critical and in the atmosphere of fictitious stress emerged information about camels, Arabs, wells, palm trees, etc, which in a sense the children never knew they knew.

Hans Furth in *Piaget for Teachers* (10) would describe this knowing as the manifestation of operative intelligence in the children's acting. Where children were consciously action, ie being a player in the drama game, they 'accommodated' to the problem which required solution. A part of a story, an incident, might offer a starting point; for example, what did the three bears say to each other after Goldilocks leapt out of the window? What would people have said at the court of the Sleeping Beauty having woken after so long a sleep? Furth continues, 'This knowing is not something that the young child... has available as a neatly packaged piece of information. It is a knowing based on experience of self and others that perhaps only a gifted writer is able to put into words. It is, moreover, a knowing that literally becomes and never exists statically, precisely because it deals with unique personal experiences.'[30]

Joan Tough distinguishes between different patterns of language; projecting, reporting, reasoning and imagining. When asked what the teacher should be doing to create situations to bring out these different patterns, and what should she be looking for and listening for, Joan Tough made this reply:[31]

'I think she needs to move in closely to the child, and talk with him and to recognise the points where she can put a comment or a question which will provoke, if you like, or promote, the child's use of language for particular purposes. She is able to check whether the child is able to respond in this way... Mostly I think we concentrate on reporting, having the child tell us about what is in front of him, but projecting through the imagination, projecting into problem-solving, doing some reasoning, are perhaps the uses that we should be concentrating on and trying to promote for every child.'

She suggests that this approach to the child should be when he is busy in an activity and when the teacher can help him to project beyond it by a 'What if...?'. The danger that it becomes merely a mechanical operation is avoided if as she says, 'the teacher is projecting into what is meaningful for the child, knowing his background and using that. Reporting on what has happened to him outside, making his own past experience important to her as a teacher.'

Here is the crux of any consideration of the teacher's responsibility for the encouragement of drama in schools. We may bring what stimuli we can, exciting and fantastic, but supremely important is the chance for the child to make 'his own past experience important to her as teacher'. All teachers' manuals must be seen against this perspective and drama manuals in particular. While the teacher assumes that it is his function to supply all the ideas, albeit culled from this or that book, then he denies the child the opportunity of being genuinely expressive. He cuts himself off from a wealth of information about where the child is in his cognitive, affective and normative development, denies himself insight into the real dynamic of the class and misses the fun of the children's invention.

With the young child the dramatic process of the organisation of his experience is obvious. Partly because there is more opportunity for him to structure his own inventions, we see a fresh expression of his understanding of the world about him. His thought processes are still overt and his responses obvious, for the issues he grapples with are simple for us to appreciate.

Drama with growing children is a more complex study. But we should not forget what experiences the child has had, what part language has played and will continue to play, and how the game of drama appears both in its structure and its dynamic.

Succeeding chapters will examine how drama relates to the child at various stages of his development and its incidence in the classroom and the curriculum.

Summary

Whereas some commentators assert that there is a difference between drama and the dramatic play of the young child, this chapter argues that there is none. It attempts to show how the young child recreates and represents experience in his make-believe play. Within his self-imposed rule structure, defined by commentary, he enjoys the same predictive satisfaction as we see displayed by adult audiences; the game with little children is discussed, while the teacher's need to be able to come to terms with less linear structured work is stressed.

Notes

[1]	Male (29) page 21	[16]	DES (54) page 7
[2]	King (69) page 11	[17]	Millar (31) page 153
[3]	Huizinga (22) page 32	[18]	DES (54) page 8
[4]	Huizinga (22) page 32	[19]	DES (54) page 106
[5]	Britton (4) page 89	[20]	DES (54) page 10
[6]	Britton (4) page 65	[21]	DES (54) page 10
[7]	Britton (4) page 66	[22]	Way (47) page 196
[8]	Britton (4) page 66	[23]	Way (47) page 196
[9]	Britton (4) page 89	[24]	Way (47) page 197
[10]	Britton (4) page 98	[25]	DES (54) page 11
[11]	Williams (50) page 38	[26]	Williamson (59)
[12]	Britton (4) page 121	[27]	DES (54) page 38
[13]	Millar (31) page 256	[28]	Goodridge (13) page 31
[14]	Slade (43) page 2	[29]	Goodridge (13) page 31
[15]	Britton (4) page 62	[30]	Furth (10) page 120

[31] Tough (53)

Further Reading

Susanna Millar (31) presents a wide range of theories that examine the role of play in the child's development. Piaget (37) and Vygotsky (46) use the language of make-believe play as a means of determining the development of thought in the young child, for they see it as the thought process in speech and action. Luria and Yudovitch (27) show this language as regulatory, a means of organising experience. Britton (4) and Barnes (2) apply these studies to the learning context of the school.

4

Drama and the Growing Child

Perhaps children in the Middle years of schooling are the most apt for drama, for this is a time of increasing social awareness, when the sum of their social experiences in the infant classroom is bearing fruit. Rule-governed behaviour supports the child's sense of identity; his role is plain amidst a set of social norms that are clear and uncomplicated. Repeatedly the cry is heard, 'It isn't fair!', for fairness is highly prized by the child of this age. Indeed, research shows that the quality most desired in a teacher by the child is fairness, not beauty, brains or wit. And by fairness, the child means adherence to the codes of behaviour upheld by consensus, and reinforced in playground games, classroom legislation, and the whole apparently solid and predictable behaviour of the adult world.

Piaget contends that there is a decline in symbolic play after the age of about four years. By this he means the very private occupation of the child in which there is such distortion of reality that what he is playing is only meaningful to himself. Reasons for this decline and ultimate disappearance include the child's increasing socialisation with its requirement of shared concepts, and the opportunities that life offers him for personal fulfilment in a social context. He adjusts to reality so that what previously was a play activity now becomes real-life situations with which he is required to cope.

The development of intelligence sees a corresponding weakening of the need for actions to stand as thoughts, the early function of play. Though this special function of play disappears, yet in games with rules we see – persisting into adult life – our preparedness to make believe, to suspend reality, and to substitute for it a world of our own making. And in drama, in particular, the recreation of experience is in order to come to terms with it, as the young child plays and does the same.

The Middle School child has largely left behind him the 'stage of intuitive thought'. To continue using Piaget's terms, he is now in the 'stage of operational thought', which means that his 'power of logical thinking is widening in range and becoming more consistent, provided that it is based on objects or situations, real, described or imagined'.[1] To strengthen and extend this 'power of logical thinking' in the context of the concrete example is the overriding aim of drama teaching in the Middle Years. The drama teacher evokes such concrete examples with the class when they ask the question 'What if...?' These 'situations which combine novelty and familiarity evoke the children's curiosity and determination to solve the problems set them'. The challenge is a real one but in a setting which is well defined and within the child's experience. Let us look at an example of a class play that illustrates how 'the drama technique not only brings out operative creativity within the child, but also carries with it a basic motivation that is intrinsic to the activity, as in the development of the intelligence'.[2] That motivation is the enjoyment of playing the drama game.

Gathered around the blackboard, a class of 'young' eleven/twelve-year-olds has created a desert island. With the help of their teacher's skilful questions, they have identified the beaches, the rocky cliffs, the palms, the fresh water springs, the volcano. As their imaginations warm to the task, they include the area occupied by cannibals and the home of 'the beast'. Their school is on old one, fifty years old at least, in a huddle of houses in the Black Country of the industrial Midlands. They would look blank if you mentioned *The Lord of the Flies*. For the teacher it is obvious that the class is intrigued with the fictional world they are creating. Their responses answer all the conditions necessary for playing a game; social consensus, submission to an invented reality, cohesion, and above all, enjoyment as the motivation. The question is, what game should they play?

At this point the teacher poses the 'What if...?' question: 'If we were a group of survivors from a shipwreck, where would we have come ashore?'. The class becomes more involved as their role changes, for they no longer have the God-like creator's view of the island, but are frightened, unhappy people who can see no further than the line of palms that edge the beach. Beyond is dark and foreboding.

The class have the knowledge of the island, and the choice is whether, as authors, they tell a story that links these survivors with the volcano, the springs, etc, or whether, as playmakers, they use the knowledge as a background to exploring the relationships between the survivors; people under the stress of a problem. The drama lesson is at a crucial stage, for will the activity be in the narrative or the dramatic mode? The class is, of course, unaware of this dilemma, but the teacher must steer the children through a clear definition of what the game is.

The teacher suggests that the class now breaks up into smaller groups, threes or fours, to decide what they see as being the most important things to be done – fetch water, build shelters, fashion weapons, etc. When they come together again it is not as school children but as survivors. They report their beliefs, they argue about priorities, they question how the tasks might be accomplished. They are not simulating the obvious characteristics – exhaustion, thirst, but are clarifying, both as participants and spectators, the problem these people have. This problem becomes apparent to the class when the teacher, who has seen it before as a potential conflict, asks them how they will determine who does what. The class respond that they must have a leader who, after some discussion, it is decided will be elected. The drama game they are decided upon, then, is an exploration of the democratic process; again, apparent to the teacher as a wider learning situation, for the children there is the fun of the unknown and unpredictable results of free choice in a vote.

The class, then, has a clear understanding of what game, but how do you play it? Excited and eager to get a result, the children quickly agree to their election procedure; everyone's name into a hat, the first four drawn out are the nominated candidates. Already ballot papers are being prepared and the hat got ready. 'What if I don't want to be leader?' someone asks. 'Put a cross by your name and if it's drawn then we'll know', is the quick response. The whole organisation is charged and the drawing of the names is done in rapt attention. Even the poorly dressed girl, not intelligent, always solitary and detached, is now with the group, for her name is also in the hat. Four names are drawn, two have crosses against them, the other two are the names of a boy and a girl. The real dynamic of the class is a very clear factor in the emerging situation, boys versus girls; the desert island and for what the leader is being chosen seem forgotten. The class is all ready to go to the final vote, anxious to know the result, though as the boys outnumber the girls it seems a foregone conclusion. But the teacher intervenes: 'How do we know', he asks, 'which one will make the better leader? How do I know which one to vote for?' The desert island is re-established, and the teacher has deepened the exploration of electoral process.

The class decide that the candidates must be subjected to a test. Each candidate, alone, will be asked the same four questions, and the answers will be analysed to indicate their resourcefulness and capability for leadership. Again the temperature rises as the candidates leave the room and the four questions are decided:

1   Where do you think we shall find water?
2   What will you do if one of us is hurt?
3   If you are hurt or killed who do you think should be the new leader?
4   What do you think is the first thing we should do?

We will remember that behind the class, on the blackboard, is the map showing water. But the class have suspended that knowledge, as later they insist that one of the candidates who glibly talks about the freshwater lake must do. This is a superb example of the dramatic process at work – players creating the illusion, not of reality, but of future consequences springing from present action; the significant present.

The candidates are brought in one at a time and the testing of them is thrilling. There is a vital feeling of the immense importance of their showing at this time; they are truly on trial. When the girl says she will make bandages, the class demand to know from what. The boy had said from palm leaves, the girl says she will tear up shirts, the class is inscrutable about both answers. Both candidates say that their successors must be similarly elected, and this seems to satisfy the class. Did they fear a dictatorship? Were they testing the potential leader's democratic principles? We shall not know, for, wisely, the teacher allowed the question, like the others, to arise from the children's logic built into the play, not from an imposed adult perspective.

Despite the protest of a boy who feels that neither candidate has answered the questions to his satisfaction, the class go to the final ballot. The girl is elected. The candidates return and the result is made known, the girl looks grave, the boy smiles sheepishly. Almost at once the bell for the end of the lesson sounds, eighty minutes has flown by and the class seem surprised to be at the end of their time. They are reluctant to leave, though it is playtime, and keep asking, 'Can we go on next time'? 'Of course,' says the teacher, 'the play hasn't really begun.' The class beam their satisfaction and depart, chattering and laughing. The teacher is right in saying the play hasn't really begun because the class have spent the time learning how to play this drama game. Next time, perhaps, if they are still interested, they will put this choice of the leader to the test, for as players they are aware of the potential hazards they face. Will the girl retain the support of the group? How will disputes be settled? What happens when people disobey orders? The teacher knows that this island is a microcosm of the human condition. All the questions that might ever be considered in a curriculum are here, in embryo.

Certainly, the teacher might expect to see the class, having identified its intention, grappling with its challenge, in role. They will play the drama game, using their knowledge as players to produce that charge that makes the significant present surrounding the characters. Above all he will see a continuation of the operational thought, so clearly visible in the lesson just gone by. New problems will arise, needing a solution in the group context.

That group will interact both verbally and emotionally, using norms and values culled from their experience to support their thinking. Truly, learning that so involves the cognitive, affective and normative in such proportion is rare. The drama game is providing that same social function that has been its purpose throughout the ages.

Some may feel that perhaps the class was side-tracked. Too much time was wasted on organisation, and the real drama – the island and its dangers – was lost sight of. But the details of the island, when they emerge, might surprise many adults. For they will reflect the class view of the situation and that may be anachronistic. Dorothy Heathcote tells the story of the boy playing the Greek guard who says, 'By gum, it's cold!'. When the class objected to the expression he changed to, 'By ye gum, it's cold!', which proved totally acceptable.

Cognitive development

The point that is being made here is a critical one, for it relates to cognitive development of children. The immense value of drama for everyone, but especially for children at this stage, is that it is rooted in the immediate and concrete example. It operates at a very low level of abstraction and therefore serves as an excellent vehicle for the thinking of children at this 'stage of concrete operations'. Recognition of these characteristics of children's thought is not only vital to any argument advocating the use of drama, but also for an undertanding of the material that will feature in the drama lesson and how it is handled.

What do we mean by 'the material', however? We cannot mean the factual content because the drama distorts any source material by its subjective selection. Therefore we cannot look for accurate reproduction of, say, a story line, a character or a particular setting. As with a still-life painting, we expect to find in the creation something more essential than the peripheral characteristics of the subject.

Clearly we are dealing with something much more than the accumulation of information, rote learning or mere accuracy of reproduction. Especially in such a creative activity we are looking for a response to stimuli drawn from concrete examples of social relations; from the life into which these children are growing and will one day influence by their decision. And that response should include their involvement in activities that, based on values and ideals, lead the children to 'grow in independence, to gain command over their feelings, to adapt to situations, to take decisions for themselves and also recognise valid authority and accept it in matters in which they lack competence'.[3]

The DES Education Pamphlet 'Towards the Middle School' (55) from which the quotation is taken, emphasises the value of the group as a context for learning. It stresses that it is the interests of the children that must form the incentive for developing skills and knowledge required by modern society. These, it suggests, are 'their ability to listen and to use the spoken word to good effect, ... to be literate, numerate and graphically competent, to possess an insight into man and society which depends on the growth of self-knowledge, on an appreciation of man's dependence on natural phenomena and resources, on some inkling of the way man has mastered his problems in the past. Children must always be encouraged to seek for meaning, for pattern and inter-connection.'[4]

The setting or situation of any dramatic piece that a class might fashion is important. But very often it is on this rock that teachers founder for they will encourage children to see them as ends in themselves. Especially is this true if the disciplines of drama and movement become confused so that the expression of the circumstances of a situation displace an involvement with its inner significance. One wonders, for example, how deeply a class would become involved in 'rescuing a fellow explorer from a dangerous tropical swamp' accompanied by *Pictures at an Exhibition* by Moussorgsky? Would the music really lead a child to 'comprehend and believe in the situation sufficiently to become minutely absorbed in it'?[5]

Such 'simple activities presented by the teacher concern only "being" something or "doing" something and do not extend to the development of a dramatic situation.'[6] Earlier the authors have suggested that 'the only control over mood is by the teacher suggesting where they (the class) are and what they are doing, or by the type of sound they can hear'.[7] In other words, by direct instruction or by manipulation through musical stimulation, the teacher totally dictates the class experience.

Now though it is intended that such work is only transitional, too often drama work in schools does not extend beyond this teacher-dominated animation. It is unfortunate that such frivolous activity should pass as drama, but much worse is that it provides support for the misconception that drama is the mere presentation of an incident as an animated narrative. For such an activity inculcates none of those resources that were mentioned in the pamphlet 'Towards the Middle School' (55); there is no educational value in work where children are denied an active role.

The setting and the situation provide starting points of enquiry, thresholds to freedom of thought and feeling. And it is this response that provides the development, the momentum of the drama work in a class. The teacher assists the class to give expression to its ideas; 'no drama teacher should look on himself as an in-exhaustible conceiver of ideas and situations. His task is, in part, to establish an area of activity within which the children can work, express, explore, invent. Once ideas are genuinely flowing, they will be self-generating'.[8] All too often the omniscient drama teacher is satisfied by the enactment of his grand plan for the class while the children proceed educationally no further than the limits of his poor invention:

'We have spent many hours in schools watching young people throw stones into rivers, walk along hot beaches, creep through haunted houses, fight against icy winds, linger at bus stops, and slide along the bottom of the sea. We have seen scores of mad scientists, writhing witches, monsters from outer space, astronauts, Indians, Polyphemoi, and intrepid explorers. Many of these exercises were far from being poor in themselves; but one missed, to repeat the point, a concept of steady development. It was difficult to perceive the area of experience the children were being required to investigate. Much was pure fantasy. But of imaginative penetration, the feeling that the children were exploring for the first time, with all their faculties alert, some area of human experience they had never known before, there was very little evidence indeed.'[9]

This lengthy quotation from the DES Drama Survey has been included because it records the actual experience of the Inspectors in many schools and because it illustrates par excellence 'the purposelessness of some of the work that was seen'.[10] Also it illustrates how totally inadequate is such aimless activity for the cognitive, normative and affective development of children at this exciting time of their growth. And one wonders how it could be that teachers, who are normally, one hopes, more sensitive to the needs of their classes, could be so myopic. Equally one wonders why children, though 'fundamentally obedient creatures',[11] should remain so tolerant in the face of the provocation of such time-wasting. Perhaps things have changed since 1968; certainly older children are less enamoured of the drama lesson than at one time.

We shall examine in a minute the answer from the teacher's point of view. The children's acceptance of such exploitation will be a partial feature of the next chapter which discusses drama in the classroom, the social situation against which any teacher has to work, within the real dynamic of the class with all its norms and hierarchies.

In Chapter 3 we talked of the necessity of the teacher 'coming to terms' with the work of the child. Now we may see this as the conflict between the formal operational intelligence and the concrete operational intelligence; knowing based on symbolic and abstract material, and knowing arising from the concrete experience directly experienced or described or evoked in words. For it is a frequent occurrence that the relevance of the subject material, obvious to the teacher and seeming effectively to define the situation, is lost upon the child, who fails to see the point of the activity demanded of him.

Too often in drama the teacher is asking children to demonstate their figurative knowledge of such experiences as those earlier described as seen by the Inspectors. That is, they were asked to show a 'knowledge that focuses on the external, figural aspect of an event in a static manner.'[12] It does not involve the child in 'a process of thinking that is operative when the child is grappling with problems.'[13] The situations did not provide the basis for the drama game, an exploration of social interaction through creating the illusion of a significant present. Viola Spolin pinpoints the connection that is trying to be made at this point when she says: 'Any game worth playing is highly social and has a problem that needs solving within it – an objective point in which every individual must become involved…'[14] The problem in the drama is always one that affects people's relationships – 'The things men do to each other, nothing more.'[15]

An example of the way in which the teacher was working at one level and the class at another, in terms of the setting, arose from a class of eight-year-olds in a school in a poor area. The teacher had attempted to evoke an experience of mountain climbing, and after much heaving and straining and mimed scrambling, which the children performed enthusiastically she announced that they had reached the summit. She now took them imaginatively, like Edgar with Gloucester in *King Lear* to the edge to look down from where they had come. Aiming at the answer of the minute size of things below, the teacher asked 'What do you see?' 'Fish and Chips' someone replied in all seriousness.

Finally in this chapter let us look at an historical event from the point of view of suggested planning in a drama 'practical handbook', and as we see it in the dialogue of a play improvised by ten-year-olds. The contrast is not merely one of material but of different ways of thinking about the event, the first concerned with presenting what we know of the details of the period in a fictitious structure, the second using the event as a base for exploring a social problem.

In *Teaching Drama* by Pemberton-Billing and Clegg[16] there are in the chapter entitled 'Planning a Drama Lesson', some suggestions for a dance drama based on the fire of London. We take up the plans at 'Beginning the story' bearing in mind that the overall aim of the work is 'to give children the opportunity of contributing their individual or small group efforts towards a class activity'.

'BEGINNING THE STORY

1   A general discussion of the fire of London, bringing out such interesting historical details as the type of fire engine (if any) that might have been used; the narrowness of the streets; the combustible nature of the buildings; the sort of clothes worn and how they might have hampered movement; water sources; etc.

2   Some practice at being Londoners going about their normal business in pairs and in small groups.

3   In this situation the fire alarm is raised – what would the immediate reactions be? Do some practical work on this to explore various possibilities.

4   A general run-through of the fire of London scene:

(a)   Londoners going about their normal business

(b)   The fire alarm is raised, and the people endeavour to put the fire   out and rescue what they can of their belongings.

(c)   The fire is over. The people return to their burnt-out homes to salvage anything that is left.

Conclusion

The teacher holds a general discussion with the class about the work they have done, and explains to them that next week they will be rebuilding London. He asks them to find out what they can about the buildings of those days; how were they constructed, etc.'

We should note that the opportunity for the class to contribute anything beyond their bodies to animate this plan is very small indeed. No wonder the Drama Report says: 'Many of the lessons seen consisted of work suggested and imposed by the teacher. "I want you to do this... I want you to do that..." were the most frequent words we heard... One longed for them (the children) occasionally to ask, why?'.[17]

The second example is from the transcript of filmed dialogue from Norwood Comprehensive School and is extensively quoted in James Britton's book, *Language and Learning*. [18] His introduction of the piece is also included.

'In the final analysis, I think the story that has been read or told, the historical facts and ideas derived from reading, visiting places, talking, and the talk of any other kind that has gone into the preparation of a dramatic improvisation – these all have similar status. They are necessary preliminaries for setting up a dramatic situation: when the improvisation gets going there comes a point at which the *situation takes over* ...

'A group of ten-year-olds from a school in a particularly depressed part of County Durham had read and talked about the Great Plague: they went on to improvise a scene in which the villagers found themselves threatened by the spread of the disease northward. A young man has been taken ill and carried into the village. Margaret, reputed to be a witch, Joanna, the young man's mother, the Beadle and the other villagers are discussing the situation. What authority has the Beadle? What rights has the young man – or his mother? What should be done to protect the village and yet care for the sick man? These are matters that the children might have considered in a class discussion – and there could have been various points of view put forward. But when the scene is enacted, the physical situation itself – the sick man lying there – pushes them to the point where something must be decided, something must be done. In interacting with each other it is to the *demands of this situation* that they are responding. These extracts (only one in this case) are from a tape-recorded transcript lasting over thirty minutes:

VILLAGER What are we going to do about it?

BEADLE We'll have him locked up, won't we?

JOANNA What do you mean you're going to have him locked up?

BEADLE Well, if he's got the plague we can't have him wandering around the streets.

JOANNA And where is he going to?

VILLAGER Yes, she thinks more about her son than us.

JOANNA Yes, maybe I do.

VILLAGER And it's better than one person dying than the whole village.

JOANNA It wouldn't worry me if the whole village *did* die.

VILLAGER No, you don't care about anyone, do you?

BEADLE Look – where are we going to put him?

VILLAGER It's no good arguing here.

VILLAGER That's Joanna's job. She's his mother.

VILLAGER Yes – you find a place to put him.

JOANNA He's going to my house – that's where he's going.

VILLAGER He's not going to your house – not next door to me he isn't.

JOANNA He's going in my house, that's where he's going!

VILLAGER He's *not* going in your house.

JOANNA Why isn't he then? You can't stop me putting him in his own house can you?

VILLAGER Not next door to *me*.

BEADLE Yes, he has his rights; he probably might get the plague.

VILLAGER I bet I will – if you go in there.

JOANNA So have I: I pay taxes on my house so I have the right to go in it, haven't I?

VILLAGER He'll have to go somewhere.

VILLAGER Yes, in an old place, somewhere away...

JOANNA Why should it be an old house? He's a *human being* not an animal!

BEADLE Well he has the plague, he's not an ordinary human being.

JOANNA That makes him different does it? So that means you can just kick him about and put him anywhere you want to? Well it doesn't to me.

BEADLE I am the Beadle.

(The Beadle orders two men to carry the son to an outlying hut.)

BEADLE Joanna has taken my orders. So *you* will take my orders.

VILLAGER *(Pause)* Come on, Peter. Let's take him.

VILLAGER I hope you get it first.

VILLAGER I doubt it, if you had hold of him.

VILLAGER Joanna, you're not going in there, are you?

JOANNA Why shouldn't I go in there?

VILLAGER Well, he's got the plague!

JOANNA Yes, and he's my son.

VILLAGER I said: are you coming in?

JOANNA Yes.

VILLAGER Then come on in.

BEADLE You'll have to stay in there!

JOANNA Who says I'll stay in? If I want to come out I will do!

BEADLE *I* say you will stay in there.

VILLAGER Yes, now *you* must take his orders.

JOANNA I don't have to do everything he says.

BEADLE It's written in the Plague Laws.

(whispering) She's going in there! She'll catch the plague off her own son!

VILLAGER There's nothing we can do, except paint a cross on the door.

VILLAGER Come on, Peter, let's go.

The teacher who wishes to be convinced that the form he has conceived for the episode is being enacted, would not enjoy the above. As in *Waiting for Godot* nothing happens, just endless talk. But anyone who examines the movement of the play in the exchanges will marvel at the skill and sensitivity with which these children play the drama game.

Summary

Perhaps among all the stages of schooling the Middle Years is the best for the teaching of drama. Not only does its process accord with the cognitive development of children of this age, but also they are most ready to work in rule-governed situations. The chapter shows how the drama should be used as a decision-making and problem-solving experience for children, and how logical thinking and abstraction can arise from the clear and concrete definition of its fiction. Above all it uses the developing communication skills of the child for increasing his awareness of the world around him. It cautions against the use of drama to show merely the results of his memory, but encourages the involvement of the child in an active learning situation that demands that he expresses his response to the source material; that he plays the drama game.

Notes

1   Educational Pamphlet 57 (55) page 8
2   Furth (10) page 123
3   Educational Pamphlet 57 (55) page 11
4   Educational Pamphlet 57 (55) page 12
5   Pemberton-Billing and Clegg (36) page 71
6   Pemberton-Billing and Clegg (36) page 37
7   Pemberton-Billing and Clegg (36) page 14
8   DES (54) page 37
9   DES (54) page 36
10 DES (54) page 36
11 DES (54) page 36
12 Furth (10) page 159
13 Furth (10) page 125
14 Spolin (44) page 5
15 Bentley (3) page 63
16 Pemberton-Billing and Clegg (36) page 119
17 DES (54) page 36
18 Britton (4) pages 146-9

Further Reading

A chapter by Dorothy Heathcote in (16) entitled 'Drama as Challenge' characterises the approach to drama adopted by many of the books mentioned above. Moffatt (32) and Martin and Vallins (30) provide classroom work in well-constructed tasks that involve the use of the dramatic process to organise and present material.

5

The Drama Lesson

In the previous chapter we examined the constraints in teaching drama that arise from the intellectual characteristics of the child in the Middle years of schooling. Now we return to the context of the classroom, with particular reference to approaches adopted by the drama teacher.

The value of such an approach to the study of the classroom and its activities is that it starts with how people behave in groups and relates the learning experience to them and their needs. Too often the subject manual presupposes a pedagogic skill that is not always possessed by the reader:

'Many books on the teaching of drama, though excellent records of marvellously creative individual attitudes full of useful suggestions, lack an introduction that identifies their underlying aim, assuming that the mere description of the content of the drama lesson will imply its intention. Unfortunately this is not always the case. These books, contrary to their authors' intentions, may provide pitfalls for the unwary who only partially understand the intentions, misapply the suggestions and, dispirited by the ensuring chaos, give up'.[1]

These very wise observations of David Male's from his *Approaches to Drama* pinpoint exactly what results when the teacher attempts to apply some of the 'good ideas' culled from the manual. But it is more than the absence of 'an introduction that identifies their underlying aim' that explains the failure of the subsequent lesson attempts. Nearer the truth may be John Holt's view of the gap between the teacher and the taught:

'Thus teachers feel, as I once did, that their interests and their students' are fundamentally the same. I used to feel that I was guiding and helping my students on a journey that they wanted to take but could not take without my help. I knew the way looked hard, but I assumed that they could see the goal almost as clearly as I and that they were almost as eager to reach it. It seemed very important to give students this feeling of being on a journey to a worthwhile destination. I see now that most of my talk to this end was wasted breath. Maybe I thought the students were in my class because they were eager to learn what I was trying to teach, but they knew better. They were in school because they had to be, and in my class either because they had to be, or because otherwise they would have had to be in another class, which might be even worse.'[2]

Motivation and task definition

This view might seem overly pessimistic, though many Secondary teachers in our Inner City schools would not think so. They would agree that the teacher's task in the classroom, and the drama teacher's in particular, might become a sight harder for experienced and inexperienced alike. The essential problem is 'that without adequate motivation there can be no adequate learning, and that adequate motivation is the function not only of intellectual clarity and perception of goals, but of satisfactory social relations between pupils as much as between pupils and teachers.'[3] The encouragement of pupils to want to learn must always be as vital a task for the teacher as his provision of what they should learn.

Now, many drama books and drama teachers assume that there is an immense reservoir of enthusiasm for drama that lies waiting to be exploited. Shipman, however, puts a contrary point of view in an article 'Order and Innovation in the Classroom' (58), a fundamental consideration for teachers using drama: 'The more a lesson departs from the traditional, the greater is the risk of disorder through lack of definition. This is why senior forms do not jump eagerly at new methods and content, for these threaten to break up secure routines, customary ways of doing things, established groupings, while simultaneously introducing the prospect of new demands for improved performance and new chances of humiliation.'[4] Then how does the drama, an unusual 'subject', get itself accepted among children? How do we steer between an imposition that is killing, and anarchy? Insights into these questions may be derived from pursuing further some of the issues raised by the writers recently mentioned. Firstly and especially important is the term 'definition', for it is a key factor in motivation, performance and evaluation. Secondly there are the interpersonal relationships in the classroom, the real climate of learning, not the expression of the teacher's anxiety for apparent pupil progress. A third issue, and perhaps sufficient for this chapter's study, is that of the organisation of the drama experience; where does it happen and for how long?

In the first chapter we explored the concept of Drama as Game and have since traced its rule structure operating in a variety of contexts. In this way we have attempted to reveal the nature of the dramatic process in order to assist understanding of its application. We have constantly reiterated the questions 'What game? How do you play it?', with the intention of using this model to come to terms with what is actually happening in the classroom. It has not been our aim to encourage the playing of parlour games in the classroom, either as a pastime, or as, reputedly, some deep educational experience. Though not denying that benefits do accrue from such activity, especially with young children, our concern has been to look at how drama as a learning experience can be identified in the life of the class.

A sure way to breed confusion is to regard the drama as innovatory as opposed to the traditional subjects. For such a view encourages one to look at only the external characteristics of the experience. Still photographs of drama lessons in schools perpetuate the euphoric celebration of the beauty of children's movement or their photogenic facial gesture. In action this arrested speech and movement can appear as more a rout than a ritual: 'When the children have resources in movement and an ear for music they usually dance. But when they have neither, their work tends to be self-indulgent and inexpressive. One head accurately described this work as 'reeling and writhing'.[5] Too often teachers are persuaded that they have successful drama work going on when they are surrounded by noisy activity. Because it appears as radically different from traditional lesson approaches, and because it can be explained as 'free expression', teachers stifle their misgivings about the educational value of the things they sanction in the name of drama.

They will confess, with relief, to a sympathetic listener that they really don't know what they are doing, much less why. Indeed, so often it is this very lack of purpose that is communicated to the class that reacts, as insecure people will, with behaviour that seeks to hide their embarrassment. To the teacher this appears as horseplay, fighting, or at best banal material culled very often from a TV series. And it must be so, for it is essentially the drama teacher's clear aim that is able to raise the interest level of the work. For the subject material may be of novel interest but novelty soon wears off. But where the material is used illustratively, a metaphoric extension of a core human experience, then its playing becomes excitingly strategic.

The following account illustrates how the original subject material, chosen by the teacher, is used by a class in a way that demonstrates their misunderstanding of the significance accorded to it by the teacher. She, responding to the level of understanding, restructures the setting to pursue the original intention more successfully. Above all, the class is taken back into the problem in terms the children can appreciate both intellectually and emotionally. The definition of the task is clear and appealing.

The teacher, influenced by '1984', introduces the idea of constant surveillance of family life by television cameras installed in every room of the house. But although the introduction has been at a level of experience familiar to the children (nosey neighbours), they have been moved too rapidly through this vital early stage of a consideration of private and public interference. It may well be that the teacher senses the class is excitable today and needs action not talk: it may be that she seems more able to handle some ebullient boys in a small group rather than in the class context. At all events, the class has been set to work exploring the concept in a domestic setting. It remains to be seen at what level they will plumb the core experience, the invasion of privacy.

The class is a secondary one in the summer term of their second year. Mainly the class divides, girls with girls, boys with boys. They sound excited, voices shrill with a great deal of noise and clumsy movement. Where a group contains both boys and girls their playing is reminiscent of adolescents in a park. They appear merely to be enjoying a game of adolescent sexual encounters. The girls are flirtatious, mincing past the smirking boys and squealing when they are grabbed and pulled down on to someone's knee. It is all good-natured and noisy, in no way sinister as the topic appeared to suggest.

After a while the teacher brings the class together to see each other's work. All the pieces have a strong sexual content: two girls invited into the flat of four men; a girl friend (played hilariously by a tough boy) apparently dispenses favours round a male family (The Homecoming?); four bored men do a striptease for the cameras installed in the house; and finally, a young woman, who covers the lens of the cameras when taking a bath, is repeatedly invaded by ogling officials. The last piece involved long simulated undressing sequences and shrill protests as the bather sought to cover her nudity with her hands.

The treatment of the material is not sophisticated. One of the boys' groups collapses at each new mention of brassiere and the class shares their humour. For these are not cool products of a permissive society but young adolescents exhibiting the major concern of the class, an increasing preoccupation with sex. In their play the cameras were treated as voyeurs rather than sinister interlopers; everything had a comic quality.

The teacher, genuinely moved by the novel, has appeared almost lost at the gap between her intentions and their realisation. The class clearly have not grasped the implications of the initial stimulus, perhaps, as its setting was so removed from their experience, it remained bafflingly abstract.

In conversation with the class, now quiet after their energetic performances, she broaches the theme once more. Really she is covering the ground lost from too brief consideration earlier in the lesson. This time she strikes a chord when she uses the example of cameras in shops to prevent shoplifting. In their eager recognition of this as a relevant experience, the class and the teacher are really beginning anew on a more clearly defined area of inquiry. The teacher has been given a second chance to explore the subject in some depth with the class.

It would be easy, but a mistake, to assume that the class had merely destroyed the teacher's intention through playing about. Equally it would be wrong to imagine that the class have created meaningfully a much more powerful expression of their own interpretation of the material. Without a clear understanding of where they were going, the class play a story line that has no more intention than to shock. Its taboos are aired, but not used with any deliberateness. The material means no more than itself, the figurative use of the roles and incidents to illustrate a dilemma in the human condition is missing; even with the reluctant bather.

The teacher did not take up any of the relationships or the incidents offered by the class in their plays. Rightly she saw that they were conceived to complete the plot, no more, and that to pursue them would have been to take the class into consideration of implications of sexual relations, for which the children were not ready. For if they are at a stage of concrete operational thinking the setting from which one starts must be within one's experience.

Many drama lessons get no further than this one did and many not as far. Certainly there are many teachers content to follow the formula of giving the idea, letting the class work on it in groups and then having them show their work – if there is time. The teacher sees his idea animated, distorted or ignored and often finds the only criticism that he has to make of the work is about the inaudibility of the players. He does not teach theatre skills but uses their deficiency as a teaching point when there seems nothing else to say. And all this springs from the fact that neither he nor the class knows how to give expression to something in disciplined dramatic form.

A typical drama lesson

Assuming this to be true, it may be useful to our examination of the working of the dramatic process to analyse the progress of a typical 'drama' lesson in social terms; what is actually happening and why.

Let us imagine that recently the newspapers and television news have featured the story of an air disaster. The teacher in planning the work for the class feels that he can rely upon the class having been exposed to the details. Therefore he decides to use as his starting point 'An Air Disaster', aimed to allow the children to use their imaginations, to work effectively in groups, and to improve their powers of communication. The method he will adopt is to introduce the topic in discussion and by asking questions assist the class to recall what it knows about air crashes both in the present situation and at other times. When satisfied that the children are involved he will set them to work in groups to explore some aspect of a plane crash – from the pilot's point of view, the passengers' behaviour, how the survivors get help, etc. Each group will show its work and the future development could put them together as scenes in a play.

The teacher has the use of the hall for thirty-five minutes, has a class of thirty ten-to-eleven-year-olds of mixed ability and with slightly more boys than girls. The class is used to this pattern of lesson and is always anxious to show its work.

As they enter the hall the class is noisy and untidy, so in order to create a more self-disciplined atmosphere, the teacher decides to try some 'warm-up' exercises. The first one involves running anywhere and 'freezing' when the cymbal is struck. The movement produces quite a few collisions and people giggle during the freeze-times. Clearly the children need a more static piece so they are put in pairs to work a mirror exercise. They have to match each other's movement without speaking. There is a great deal of talking and laughter and the imitation is not accurate. There is a feeling that this is a very familiar exercise for the class and one which does not provide much interest any more. The teacher feels that valuable time is slipping away and that perhaps it would have been better to have started as he had originally intended. So he stops the class and calls them to sit round him. The proximity of the boys sitting closely in a tangle of children leads to horseplay which the teacher resolves by separating the offenders.

His questions quickly produce from the children the focal point he requires. They have much more information than he requires and having appeared to be soliciting their knowledge of the recent disaster he is constrained to allow more random talk than he really wants or time allows. So he cuts through the wealth of information that the raised hands and voices represent, to announce that they are going to make their own disaster. When he dismisses them, he tells them that they must form a group and work out whether they are the crew, the passengers, ground control, etc. The class is already full of planning talk while he is still dealing with a boy who is asking if it is alright if he is the hijacker who makes the plane crash. Although that was not his intention, the teacher allows this as the class is already moving away into noisy bunches. The parted combatants now reunite and immediately begin to wrestle as hijacker and guard. Indeed an alarming number of the boys seem to have cottoned on to that idea. Where a quieter group are simulating the cabin and the controls they are set upon by another group of lusty hijackers. This is not part of their plan and they protest ultimately to the teacher as they are not as strong or as numerous as their attackers. The teacher stops the class and warns the children that they will not be allowed to make their play if they don't behave. He sorts out the groups and sets them to work once more, making sure that the difficult boys are settled to plan their piece. He has even suggested to them that they are the survivors, dazed and injured who have to find help. The boys are excited by the prospect and soon the teacher feels able to leave them to get on by themselves.

The rest of the class is busy, not apparently working to a plan but making it up as they go along. They shout instructions to each other as the noise is intense. They have set out chairs more or less elaborately and these clatter over as the crash occurs in different parts of the hall. The teacher is aware that the noise level is such that it might invite intervention of the headmaster and also the time indicates that only seven minutes are left. He stops the class and asks them to sit down to watch their pieces. Talk immediately resumes and this he quells, stressing that they have to pay attention to the scenes of others to be able to criticise them, especially as they will put the scenes together to make a play. As some semblance of quiet is apparent he invites the naughty boys' group, with which he had planned, to show theirs first. The piece starts as he might expect with the survivors reeling about like drunken men. But soon a dispute about food and water arises and the exhausted men fight with remarkable energy. Already people are walking through the hall and embarrassed by what appears as riot, the teacher stops the piece. As he asks for the next, the bell rings and amid cries of frustrated actors, the chat of the naughty group, the increasing horde invading the hall and the clatter of the dinner ladies, he promises they will see the rest next time.

Nothing worked as he had planned, he feels exhausted and depressed because the idea was a good one. He dare not evaluate the lesson because the lofty aims remain as an indictment of his ability to produce drama with the class. For the children there is no such heart-searching. In the playground they are doing much the same as they were previously doing in the hall. The lesson was very much as usual with the opportunity for some fun and a break from the more formal task of writing. As usual, one had to make up a story about a given idea, and act it with friends – if there was time. 'Sometimes it get boring when you have to do the same idea again or when you have to do the same thing, like being mirrors, and that'. To be honest neither class nor teacher could really justify the work to an anxious mother, irate father or sceptical deputy head.

This imaginary incident might seem a cruel exaggeration of an unfamiliar scene; it is not. Its details are fictional, but the experiences they exemplify have been seen again and again. And worse, where the work is concluded and shown, too often the teacher is satisfied by that fact alone and does not seek to question the substance or the progress of the lesson.

Nor should we dismiss such people as merely bad teachers. Our teacher in the made-up incident could read the class, he knew that their response was not what he, nor they, really wanted. What eluded him was the understanding of how to satisfy their needs dramatically. Both he and the class shared immensely confused expectations; the blind leading the blind.

In what way might the luckless teacher here described have been assisted by the idea of his drama lesson as game?

The post mortem
The first consideration must be of his aims; were they too ambitious? The answer must be that they were not, and that to work for an imaginative response, to have it shaped by the group and communicated in a conscious expressive form, was merely to use the dramatic process. But was it that the time was too short? Can all these things happen in a lesson of that length? Again the answer must be, yes, if the teacher and the class are clear about what game they are playing. Let us consider an analogy drawn from another familiar activity. The teacher who is taking a class for a game of rounders, for example, does not spend valuable time inviting his pupils to guess what game he has in mind for them to play. The intention is clear to all and their energies are employed in making the conduct of the game possible in the time by organisation and clear decision-making. Too often, drama teachers, though aware of the area they intend exploring, pretend that the field of inquiry is in fact an open one.

In this example the questioning, following the abortive and unrelated concentration exercises, increased the excitement of the class, provoking reactive and not reflective behaviour. The teacher's first task was either to have abandoned his plan and instead to have worked the class vigorously in a physical way to meet that need, or to have settled them down in more conventional ways. As it was he fell between all stools and was never able to create a suitable climate for creative work. Had he clearly and honestly introduced his intention of making a play about an air disaster then the class contributions might have been selectively employed to assist that intention. Furthermore the class might have offered far better ideas than his for the conduct and outcome of their activities, especially if pressed by the urgency of the time constraint.

To write thus of a lesson might appear to be advocating the obvious to a degree of banality. And it is true that there is nothing startling in the suggestions made, but that is just the point, that essentially the drama lesson is like others on the curriculum. It does not require any special set of procedures nor the sort of unusual behaviour that some warm-up exercises suggest as a prerequisite. Above all, the awareness that was essential for a successful exploration of the topic was not to be derived from just a vigorous, physical experience. Essentially the dramatic potential in the subject resides in how the particular circumstances affect people's relationships in an abnormal way. Perhaps it would be more true to say that the area that intrigues in this game, as maybe in any other, involves attempting to establish normality amid the abnormality of the game's constraints. We do not merely pretend that constraints do not exist, but play with such skill that they provide no obstacles to our design. So the exhilarating game of rugby football is one that not only transcends the restrictions that its rules would impose, but actually is improved immeasurably by the efforts required to do so. In the game of the air disaster, success might have been achieved by the eventual establishment of some sort of social order amidst the chaos of the accident. The interest is held by the continued requirement to adapt normal behaviour to accommodate to the unusual circumstances, but at the same time to retain sufficient familiar features to maintain social cohesion.

What else could one attempt to do with such a theme? A novel could dwell upon the plane's impact and the immediate horror, though *Lord of the Flies* did not. A film could show us pictures of the interior and exterior of the aircraft during its terrible descent and upon the ground. But the drama cannot produce events of such magnitude except in human terms, that is, as they affect a person in relation to his fellows. So the awful descent of the plane is seen in the behaviour of the passengers, in their heroism or selfishness. The aftermath, equally, can be explored only by narrowing the whole focus of the inquiry so that it appears in the same human terms. And, strangely, this apparent reduction of scale into more familiar features has an opposite effect. The tragedy is in fact perceived with a greater awareness, the universal significance revealed in the particular example through the metaphor of drama.

The teacher in this example did not succeed, perhaps because he neglected to give in the inquiry period of the lesson a sense of the challenge of the material. In words, in movement or in music, for example, he needed to take his class beyond the sensation of this most recent air disaster. Human disaster is the same in all circumstances; only the details are different. This concept should perhaps have been explored so that it could provide the background against which a particular event could have been presented. And though this may sound high-flown and over-ambitious, some sense of it all could be achieved in experiencing the playing of the breaking of bad news, encountering death, the anxiety of awaiting news of lost relatives. Such encounters may delay the grand design if one thinks only of the incident in epic terms. If, however, we believe that they can assist perception, then they might exemplify what Albee suggests in *The Zoo Story* (1) when he says, 'It's one of those things a person has to do; sometimes a person has to go a very long distance out of his way to come back a short distance correctly.'[6]

The teacher and the class will always perceive the lesson differently if the teacher is really performing his function properly. The child will see the activity as interesting for its own sake. In other words he will not be conscious of the educative value of the process, or necessarily of how the work relates in the widest sense to his immediate school future, or to the more distant future that will embrace him once he leave school. A partial understanding there must be, in order to provide motivation for the work – a crucial question for drama teaching where often there seems very little reason for behaving so unnaturally. But long-term goals are not sufficient incentive, as every teacher knows, and it is his task to provide more immediate satisfaction for his pupils without being merely a childminder.

For the child, the drama lesson should offer him the opportunity of exploring and communicating his response to a problem in human relationships. As a task it differs from other studies in Humanities in that it must always be primarily inductive. The exercise is firmly rooted in the concrete example which is represented by the actual body, and by emotional responses to unreal stimuli. It moves to a perception of universal truths, to knowledge, through creating a living present, the substance of which relies for its continuance upon consensual recognition of the human norms and values it portrays. Where the child regards the process as Game, then, as with any other game, the playing of it 'is highly social and has a problem that needs solving within it – an objective point in which every individual must become involved'(44). The payoff from drama arises from using one's social skills strategically to create a dynamic picture of the way people behave.

The task in drama

For the teacher, too, the drama lesson serves the same educational end. The furtherence of his pupils' knowledge through the organisation and communication of their experience in the dramatic process must be his major aim. The actual material is less important; we should not be too concerned about cliche, but the group dynamic is vital. By this is meant the actual relationship of the teacher to the class and the pupils to each other. We might now profitably take some time to examine the drama lesson in this context, analysing what is the nature of the task and how it is tackled.

It would appear incontrovertible that drama is a very active learning experience. It is often referred to as a 'practical' subject, not as opposed to impractical subjects, but, unfortunately, as opposed to 'academic'. The use of the word 'practical' suggests learning through doing, less instruction, indeed a departure from a formal teacher-dominated situation. We would anticipate that such a learning situation would allow discussion, controversy and equality of opinion. And for such dialogue to happen in any meaningful way, the relationship between the teacher and his pupils and among the pupils themselves, would be reflected in the more informal use of space.

Now, these conditions do not distinguish practical and non-practical activities, though they are characteristic of the 'practical'. Essentially they reflect an approach that acknowledges the classroom as a social group. How the teacher and the pupils interact will take many forms, each of which will be appropriate to a given task, will satisfy (or express) a particular need. It cannot be said, therefore, that any one form is the best in all circumstances.'[7] The major forms of interaction may be set out thus:[8]

1 Teacher-centred, task directed, autocratic with passive learning.
2 Teacher and task centred, autocratic, moving in the direction of co-operation and active learning.
3 Pupil and task-centred active learning.
4 Group-task centred active learning.

The categories illustrate the extremes of the teacher's role, from dominance to virtual non-existence of traditional status. However they are not set out as representing a progress from bad to good teaching. Which situation should be encouraged at any time in a classroom will depend 'on the needs and tasks of the moment'. 'It is, however, of great importance that the teacher should be clearly aware of the sort of situation he is in, and why, and change it for reasons connected with the *task* and the changing needs of pupils and not for reasons connected with his own status or need to be dominant.'[9]

Drama teachers sometimes find it difficult to define what situation they are in, because they are confused about the task upon which the pupils are engaged. This confusion arises partly from not separating the long and short term aims of the work, partly from insufficient understanding of methodology. And the two combine when, for example, such lesson aims as 'the encouragement of self-expression, freedom of expression in speech and movement and creative language and movement', assume that the teacher never interferes in or influences the children's work.

Such aims as those quoted are undeniably desirable and can be fostered in very positive learning situations, but not where there is merely a negation of control. It takes skill to create opportunities for children, free of external constraints, to be governed by a self-discipline arising from their response to material potentially dramatic.

The teachers, real and imaginary, whose lessons we examined, each began with strictly teacher-centred approaches. But before the benefits of this relationship with the class could show themselves, they transferred authority for an ill-defined task to groups who were still impotent through ignorance. For when the task that is given to a group is aimed at encouraging decision-making and problem-solving, then there must be real decisions arising from genuine, recognised problems. The problem for the group may well be to present the teacher's vision, but they must be aware that that is what is wanted. For example, the first teacher might have said, 'There are concealed cameras in each room and the family know they are there. Let each group be a separate family and let each *show their response* to this loss of privacy'. Now, here, the teacher has decided what is to be done and why. For the class the learning experience involves creating a significant present for the family from their own recollections of loss of privacy. They learn to use their own experience symbolically to communicate, to share, an insight into the human condition.

It is common, though, for teachers to encounter work initiated by the children themselves. In drama it happens when the class ask whether they might be allowed to do their own play: 'Please Miss, can we make up our own play today?' The question often causes the teacher an anxious moment, and in some manuals that have a section devoted to the questions that teachers ask, this dilemma often appears. They wonder how far they should allow such work, particularly as it results in play that is 'endless, timeless, shapeless and unselective'. Teachers expect to find a form at least, a comment at best, clearly defined characters and, above all, a good plot. Rarely do these appear, and the anarchic knockabout that is shown seems to threaten the teacher both as an authoritarian and as an instructor.

That the work should emerge thus is a clear indication of the negation of the teacher's role. For although the class may be clear about its goal, the means of achieving the end the children desire may well lie with the teacher. The procedures he suggests might, even if rejected, provoke other thoughts, and perhaps better thoughts, about how to make the play. It is a situation in which the teacher must come to terms with what the class is seeking to create. He will only be successful in his teaching if he is able, through this perception, to assist his pupils towards a satisfactory form for the expression of their ideas.

Though this is easy to say, it is more difficult to put into practice, unless one is aware of the process that is operating. What is the learning that is taking place and how does it occur?

Learning through drama

What happens in drama is a process that involves perception and expression. They are not separate experiences but are linked, so that perception is gained through expression and the expression is, itself, the communication of understanding. However, it is possible to recognise when the drama is being employed in an exploratory way, a discovery of common meanings by which people live in a community. Such understanding is derived from the heightened awareness of the power of language and movement to make such meanings from the organisation of group experience. Take, for example, the play of the children about the Plague that was transcribed at the end of the previous chapter. In the dialogue we can discern how the children, in role, use their own experience of authority, motherly love, indifference, etc, in the game of drama. That the players are able to respond to each other, to follow and sometimes initiate moves, arises from their recognition of the aptness, the truth, of the recollected experience, and how it marries with their own. Their response, in turn, extends the relationships that are the substance of the encounter, and stimulates the original player to further moves. Together the players affirm the insights they have into human behaviour and how it is socially evaluated. By playing out the lives of others, they re-examine their own, and always in relation to the norms and values of their community. Nor are their means merely those of language, though it is the most important, but also the social meaning of movement. Spatial relationships are discovered to be crucial, the interpretation that people put upon facial and bodily gesture. And all this happens in a genuine atmosphere of discovery when the players submit themselves to the rules of the game and accord it the seriousness that must attend any game.

As the exploratory function of the drama is clearly discernible, so is the communicative. This happens when the actors wish to share their insights with others who have not been party to the whole experience. They are required to use their role encounters symbolically, so that language now becomes important for its pitch, pace, pauses and timbre, and movement becomes gestural, an extraverbal language. The selection of the symbols by the actors makes the encounters significant to the audience. They, in turn, are required to be alert, so that they may, by their recognition, confirm for the actors the truth of their social model. For if the players represent a set of human relationships that are far removed from common experience, the spectators will react only with a baffled incomprehension, which will, in turn, affect the sharpness of the actors' performance and ultimately create nothing meaningful. The reiteration of the phrase, 'in turn', demonstrates how the progress of the drama game is dependent on this two-way exchange that represents the genuine process of community; a shared understanding of the bases of social order.

It must be apparent in the very language that is being used that there can be no division between the exploratory drama and the communicative function, theatre. Both employ the same essential dramatic process, but differ in the degree of constraint attending them. Inevitably, the task of communicating with others in a traditional form will be more complex, and theatre as a social institution reflects just such complexities. As the game involves a wider number of people, then its conduct must allow for all participants, both actors and audience. And there should be no embarrassment about using the term 'acting'. It denotes merely the way in which the game is played; the adoption of role, the strategic use of verbal and non-verbal communication skills, the creation of a virtual present. Now, this process occurs whether the drama is being used as an exploration or as communication. Moreover, the recognition of the process as the conscious application of skills is vital for the teachers' appreciation of the stages of the drama lesson. We know where we are if we are clear about how the game is played.

With this analysis of the way drama works as a learning experience, it is possible to express the progress of a drama lesson in diagrammatic form. This can show both the means employed by the group and how the ends they achieve constitute the game of drama. It does not represent what should happen necessarily in any one lesson; it is not a lesson plan moving from Aims to Evaluation in thirty-five minutes or so. Instead it sets out a possible movement from drama as an exploratory method to its use to communicate to others than the players themselves. Whether the class

PERCEPTION

1 Inquiry
Exploring an idea
verbally, visually
aurally

Is game possible?

2 Decision
Arriving at an
understanding of the
group's intention

What is the game?

3 Definition
The intention explored
in action

How do we play
the game?

· · · · · · · · · · TO PERCEIVE RELATIONSHIPS · · · · · · · · · · ACTING · · · · · · · · · · TO EXPRESS THE RELATIONSHIPS · · · · · · · ·

EXPRESSION

4 Committal
Declared relationships
in action

Playing the game

5 Reflection
Redefining the
problem

Looking back on
game

6 Appraisal
The teacher evaluates the experience. Did the game assist the learning process?

progress through the complete movement will depend upon many factors; time, the clear definition of the goals and how to achieve them, social cohesion, etc. We will remember the children, playing the survivors on the island electing a leader, who took eighty minutes defining the government of the island. It would only be at a subsequent time that they might commit themselves to the relationships they had evolved through their electoral choice. They used drama to define the problem of lack of leadership, the island with them as survivors was merely a setting for the more universal social dilemma. The consequences of their decision would provide yet another area for inquiry should it prove of interest to the group. The communication of insights gained from both might form the core of a play that they might construct and present to another class, parents or some other people not party to the original exploration. This might express the changing fortunes of leaders, like Long John Silver, or the agony of unpopular decision, like Ralph's in *Lord of The Flies*.

Perhaps the most valuable explanation of the model will be gained by analysing the progress of a drama session closely relating it to the plan shown in the diagram.

A class of some twenty-four boys of about eleven to twelve years of age are assembled in the corner of the hall/gymnasium of an old school in a poor part of a Midland city. They sit on gymnasium benches in a square, and behind them the rest of the space lies empty and impersonal. The teacher sits among the boys quietly waiting for any latecomers and allowing the din of lessons changing over to subside. The boys talk to each other in subdued voices as they catch the feeling of calm and self-control that the teacher is generating. Although the atmosphere is perhaps less formal than in other classes, nevertheless there is no conscious attempt to create a totally different approach to the work, at this stage. What distinguishes this from, say, a maths lesson will appear in the process the class employ to organise their experience, not in freedom from classroom restraints or non-intellectual treatment of learning.

The Inquiry

The teacher tells the boys that it is his intention that they will make a play. What he says, is in fact, 'Good, now today we are going to make a play', and the class reaction is neutral; they are neither for nor against the idea at this juncture. This is because the idea is too abstract, a play too far removed from the everyday experience of most of them. The teacher knows this and amplifies the definition of their task with an explanation of Dorothy Heathcote's. 'A play is just a problem for a number of people. Now, there are twenty-four people here, so we have to find a problem for twenty-four people. But first let's agree whether our play will be something that happened long ago or in modern times. Think for a minute and then we'll vote on it.' The class show by a majority of raised hands that they favour modern times. One boy wished to be allowed to include the future but the teacher says not on this occasion. He abstains from voting altogether and the teacher does not insist. What is happening is the establishment of the rules of the drama game, a consensual structure for the living present they will ultimately construct. They are about to take the first major step towards that creation with an exploration of ideas, *the Inquiry stage* of the session.

The boys are requested to make groups to two, three or four and to decide upon a problem for twenty-four people living in modern times. Soon they are called together again and each group reports its ideas; an apartment block that catches fire, a plane crash, a hijacking, an epidemic, a bank raid, etc. Each time the teacher assists the group to define clearly what is the dilemma not simply as narrative but how the problem might affect individuals. For example the plane that is hijacked has a critically sick person abroad and delay will cause his death and this pressurises the airport control.

Two boys have a less predictable problem. 'Well, you see, sir', they say, 'there's these fishermen and something white comes out of the water and goes past them and disappears in the graveyard.' 'Yes', replies the teacher, 'but what is the problem?' 'It's a ghost', the class, not only the originators, cry, as though the teacher is pitifully dense not to have appreciated that. 'I know that', he replies 'but are there twenty-four fishermen, and if so, what is their problem?' There is a short silence as the boys think this over, for their play had been conceived for the two of them alone, and this is unacceptable. Then one of the boys says, 'Well, they belong to this club, see?' The teacher who is not a fisherman, does not see. He presses for more detail but the boys find it difficult to articulate the dilemma. But because he respects that they see the import of the incident, the teacher does not dismiss their contribution but tries to penetrate the world that the child so clearly envisages. Then, suddenly, he appreciates the point and marvels at his blindness, for where but in a fishing club in which incredulity is most common, could it be more difficult to convince people that one had seen a ghost? The dramatic potential of the idea is staggeringly forceful, the humour rich, and all the conditions of the task, at least at this stage, fulfilled.

Even though he sees this potential, the teacher attempts to allow impartiality. But the class, too, are taken with the idea and overwhelmingly elect to make their play on this theme. The drama game is possible, for there has been a seriousness about the suggestions, accompanied by responsible choice. Also the idea appeals to the class, so that the element of enjoyment that is vital to the conduct and the persistence of games players is evident. Often teachers spend, and rightly so, a whole session with routines to establish obedience to the rule demands of drama. The drama game cannot even be defined, much less played, until such conditions exist. Gavin Bolton called it 'getting ready for drama', and many manuals suggest lessons as drama lessons that are no more than that; which is not to deride them, nor to deny the essentiality of control, either within the material or imposed by the teacher. For as with any game, violation of the rules makes it 'a poor thing'. But we must recognise that although such obedience creates the opportunity for playmaking, it is not itself the drama.

The decision

The teacher has established which theme the class will work upon, but he does not assume that the clarity of the one boy's vision, nor now his own, is common to all. But he questions the class about the ethos of the club, the activities, how its members would respond to surprising news, etc. So that *the Decision* amounts not merely to faint support but to a genuine understanding by all of the group's intention; they are all aware that the game they are playing is the same game. This need not appear as an explicit agreement but may be implicit in the questions the class might ask, their comments and suggestions. Above all the teacher's task is to assist the clarity of their intention and to support their construction even by playing the devil's advocate or by requiring to be reassured on certain points about the scenario: Not the story, but the setting for an exchange of human relationships.

The definition

As with the desert island lesson the most critical time came when the teacher steered the work to the dramatic and not the narrative, so, now, the class needs to clarify their statement of the problem *in action*. This period of the lesson cannot be over-emphasised in its importance, for it represents the application of the dramatic process; playing the drama game, to perceive through the interaction of the people represented, truths concerning social relationships. It reveals what the core of the play is about, what set of relationships provides the rules of this particular game. *This period of Definition*, on this occasion, takes the form of the boys making the setting of the club. The impersonal space of the hall is now given specific characteristics, not elaborately with scenery, but by a consensus that agrees upon the significance of that area. Like parts of a playing field that have strategic importance, the playing area becomes the preserve of different groups; the darts players, the card players, the talkers, bragging about catches, and the teamaker's galley. Anyone coming into the hall would not immediately recognise the setting, for he would not be party to what it was intended for – the problem of convincing the sceptic. But the boys know not only how their varied grouping provides an immediate tapestry of personalities and interests, but also how there is within their cynical rivalry a problem for the ghost-seers, the game's main issue. This perception arises from their natural ability to use their social experience to define social situations, and now they use the skill creatively.

The teacher's function at this time is to 'coach' the players in those social communication skills that they are using selectively, and to ensure that the play does not become too diffuse. On this occasion, for example, he may visit the darts players asking them how they feel about the gaggle of braggarts loudly destroying concentration for others. So he may relate their activity to others in the room and maintain the corporate aim and method. Very interestingly he enabled the child, unaccepted into any group, to be part of the setting by being teamaker. This role gave him licence to be part of every group but in a strictly defined way. At all times the observations are expressed in a dramatic way, they are proven in actual interaction of persons.

When the ghost-seers arrive, everyone has become too concerned with his own activity and the general setting of byplay, so their entry passes virtually unnoticed and their attempts to gain attention fail. The game will now lose its way unless its essential purpose is maintained. But the teacher does not bang a gong or provide some other outside control to signal their entry. Instead he stops the playing, for to do so is acceptable and, as would be the case with any game, is not in any way destructive if it is genuinely for clarification. Together the class then decide why in such circumstances the members of the club would pay attention. The teacher may have his own ideas but it is the class, and only they as club members, who can provide the answer. In this case the boys agree that the two who have seen the ghost are the Club President and Secretary and, therefore, because they often have to give out notices and address everyone, are listened to 'when they get up on the stage'. So a technical detail is settled but in the terms of what is being created and in a way that ensures the momentum of the game. They try it out and it works to everyone's satisfaction, it feels right for that's what people do. 'Now, lads, gather round, me and the Secretary have something to say', and in more or less reluctant haste the club assembles, still discussing the controversy of their activities, eventually to fall silent. Then how dramatic the announcement, so unexpected, with its derisive reception, 'Oh, get away, did you stop us just for that! etc.' The Definition is clearer by the class being taken back, in this case by intervention, to the Inquiry and the Decision. But in the playing, too, there is this recycling, a proof that all the stages are not sequential but recurrent as the need for their functions reappears.

The Committal

Bit by bit, the plan is played out, to a point where the original idea is realised. In a sense the original core idea, the relating of the ghost experience, has been so worked upon that it becomes a dramatic experience, not a narrative one; it eventuates from a number of social encounters. Almost imperceptibly the class enter the *stage of committal* where those relationships, implicit in the original conception are now expressed explicitly in the progress of the game. The payoff of this game, the most thrilling part for the class and the teacher, is the interrogation when all players are alert. For example the ghost-seers, pressed for proof cite the leaving of their rods behind 'with a fish on the hook', as strong confirmation. The class are impressed immediately, the teacher, only on reflection, realises that only in very exceptional circumstances would a fisherman abandon his rod, much less his catch. The boy who wanted a play about the future, though working conscientiously, had never really submitted to the majority choice and now remains the most obdurate sceptic. A bright little boy, so anxious as to be the class clown, suddenly announces that he, too, has seen the ghost some days earlier. His confession is meant to support the story but support from this quarter is more a liability. But he wins admiration as a player when he is confronted with why he hasn't spoken before. His reply that he lacked the strong proof of these recent reports, brilliantly clears him and supports them, an adroitness greeted with jeers of approval. Here we see the same response as when team mates admire an unexpected piece of fine play by one of their weaker members and hoot from the pavilion.

The class shapes the piece by making plans to meet the next day at the river bank, a decision hastened by the fact that the time for closing has arrived. The members leave chatting, chaffing, marvelling, while the teamaker collects the cups and begins to sweep the floor, a detail that pleases the class again with its rightness. A reaction worthy of noting, for by that time they had become the audience, appreciating, unconsciously, the significance of the gesture.

The reflection and evaluation

The boys return to the benches where their teacher sits. They are excited by their achievement but relaxed, a mood the teacher uses to conduct the *reflection*. The players discuss what worked and what didn't and why, the difficulty of convincing people without proof, and how the people they had created would react to the climax or anticlimax that the morrow could prove. The teacher does not labour this stage but allows the class to enjoy its success. Nevertheless what he has seen and heard will affect his own *evaluation* of their progress in using drama to express and explore, and what yet needs to be encouraged. Above all he will have remarked how well or how badly they have used their social skills and how he might assist them here. For they will need these tools for all their lives. And it may occur that as a result of today the teacher decides to conduct a more teacher-centred piece of work to achieve a distinct result which would result from efficient use of verbal skills.

The role of the teacher over the eighty minutes has been that of a teacher of any subject, as the class experience also has been the same perception and expression as other classes following other subjects. What has been different has been the way of learning, an active application of their resources in a game model; a learning by being.

Summary

This chapter examines the classroom as a social situation, a group learning experience with all the attendant characteristics of group behaviour. The approaches of the teacher and his understanding of the nature of the pupils' task are regarded as perhaps the most vital factor. An analytic model of the drama lesson is introduced and related to an account of a drama lesson. It illustrates where the teacher's input is essential and where he should hold back and all this in the context of game-playing.

Notes

1 Male (29) page 17
2 Holt (21) page 37
3 Oeser (34) page 82
4 Shipman (58)
5 DES (54) page 32
6 Albee (1) page 164
7 Oeser (34) page 52
8 Oeser (34) page 53-5
9 Oeser (34) page 59

Further Reading

Shipman (41)
Holly (20)
Male (29)
Oeser (34)
Skinner (42)

Slade (43)
Way (47)
Pemberton-Billing
  and Clegg (36)
NATE (57)

There are a number of manuals suggested in this chapter – Male (29), Pemberton-Billing and Clegg (36), Slade (43) and Way (47) – which contain activities for drama in the school. They have often implied considerations of group dynamic and teacher/pupil interaction within their practice. Oeser (34), Shipman (41), and Skinner (42) are explicit about these relationships and form a useful commentary to the classroom manuals. Holly (20) and Heathcote (57) equate the two against a background of experience, scholarship and common sense.

6

Drama and the Multicultural Classroom

The demands made upon the teacher in the multicultural classroom are legion, and it would be understandable if such a teacher were to throw up his hands at the suggestion of drama as an additional activity. For it is likely that drama would be regarded by him as an optional extra, or at best an aid to language acquisition for non English speaking children of immigrant parents. This chapter, however, seeks to assert that this learning tool is essential to such children, being rooted in the concrete experience, involving the child's language at his own developmental stage, reinforcing the relationship between the child and his teacher who as often as not is of another culture, and, finally, assisting the teacher to gain insights not only into the child's unconscious concerns but also into his cultural and social values and norms.

A major difference of opinion exists over what is the most advantageous education for children of minority ethnic groups. The process of assimilation of such children into the dominant culture has obvious disadvantages, although should they wish to enjoy its benefits or a career they need to be able to compete on equal terms with all others. However, the loss of their own identity and the immersion in predominantly cognitive learning experiences that deny the affective balance of their own backgrounds, is an impossible price to pay. Their learning materials will reinforce this difference using, as they do, examples and illustrations from an alien experience, while the language of instruction will often ignore their own, and sometimes positively forbid its use.

The argument for separate development to preserve cultural identity and traditional values is one that must evoke sympathy but it, too, has its disadvantages. One of these, the career prospects view, has already been mentioned, but there are others that are more persuasive. These must involve a social perspective that is more universal, and such a concept of the social process was examined earlier.

The view of social reality was agreed to be a transient experience, constantly reconstructed by people through their social exchanges. The health of a community, it was argued, invoking Williams's terms, lay in its ability to discover 'common meanings and common means of communication'. And no matter what view is taken, a multicultural society involves people sharing their living space as a very minimum requirement.

For the child of immigrant parents yet born in the country of adoption, there is the constant cultural conflict especially with the immensely pervasive influence of the media. Teenage fashions in dress and music, for example, do not only mark the non-participating adolescent as culturally different in a national sense, but also, perhaps more painfully different from his very peer group. The problems that arise from relationships between the sexes and across the cultures are not ones which can be eliminated by ignoring them or indeed forbidding them.

The pluralist society

Some might well say that such social problems beset any society, multicultural or not, and are only exacerbated when there is an ethnic mix. They would argue that among any social group one could find a wide range of beliefs, attitudes and practices and that what we should be aiming for is a pluralist society. This should encourage diversity, and promote, certainly through its education, tolerance through genuine mutual respect and understanding, not a uniform acceptance of any one position.

One of the ways in which such an ideal can be realised is through honest appraisal; the opportunity both to celebrate and to challenge prevailing social norms and values. Such an opportunity, it is argued throughout this book, lies in the drama and the social models it constructs for examination. Uniquely it can provide a vital, expressive meeting point for people of differing views and backgrounds. Their submission to a common created reality allows reflection but, because of the game features, does not require or even imply a fundamental change of opinion, only the common consent to play the Drama Game.

I recall the drama invention of a class of nine to ten year old children, most of Asian extraction, in an inner part of a Midland city.

The class has been invited to suggest starting points for playmaking. The list is predictable and includes Robbing a Bank, War, Murder, Magic, Dangers in the Snow, Hi-jacking, Bombs and Terrorists, Volcanoes, Famine. The teacher explores with the class each suggestion then lists the contributions and then puts them in sets – Lawbreakers, Natural Disasters, The Supernatural, etc. This ensures that everyone's suggestion is accepted but that there is not such enormous diversity that consideration of them becomes too diffuse.

Next the class is asked which set it prefers and by an overwhelming majority 'Lawbreakers' wins the vote. Rather than attempt a further selection from within this group of suggestions, and in order to avoid a more narrative invention, the teacher declares his interest in the play. 'We all know', he says, 'how people break the law, for it is the usual stuff of television. What interests me is not *how* people break the law but *why* people break the law. Especially interesting is why people, who know a law is to be obeyed, as a group should decide to break it. Can you think of examples of such people who knowingly and deliberately break the law?'

Unlike the previous responses which often consisted of single words, the children now are descriptive and cite a group of overtaxed villagers or an edict that prevent newcomers entering a country. In all cases the reason for violating the law resides in its moral unacceptability. The raw material of the drama lesson has been identified and the Inquiry stage almost imperceptibly moves towards the articulation by the class of its Decision of what the Drama Game is to be. There is a President who makes a new law which overtaxes people and which denies entry to the country, lest opponents to his regime further disaffect an already angry populace.

The teacher who has encouraged discussion for some time and has that guilty feeling that the children ought to be 'doing something' releases them too early to exploring some of the history of these people by simulating their village life. The class with great gusto transform the classroom into shops and houses with energetic but purposeless play. The entry of a messenger from the President interrupts this play, a cause of real resentment that manifests itself in noisy rejection of the child messenger's news and near riot. The play that was identified earlier was not lost because a more acceptable alternative emerged, but because the Definition, the concretisation of the implications of 'The President's New Law', was never pursued, as a result of the teacher's ineptitude.

On a subsequent occasion the teacher pursued the question of Deliberated Lawbreaking in role play. Here acceptance or rejection of persuasion to break a law was the keynote of pair or group improvisation. It was not the act, but the consenting to the act for acceptable reasons, that was explored by the class. The rules governing such a Drama Game were familiar to them and produced original and perceptive encounters. Everyone's exchange was seen and used as examples of behaviour that excited comment because of the expressed social values. Collectively these encounters represented a number of attitudes and focused attention upon the responsibility that accompanies a decision either to accept or reject a legal constraint.

The ground had now been broken for a return to the play and the class, in another lesson, were invited to consider further the circumstances surrounding 'The President's New Law'.

The scenario that emerged was more precise and with seeds of dramatic intensity: each year the President issues a new law, the details of which are conveyed to the communities within his realm by a messenger. This year his edict denies the right of entry of any new people into the country.

The teacher explores verbally with the children what the effects of such a law would be for people, and learns of the widow who is denied the promised and expected return of her son; a man who has incurred debts and has promised to clear them with the money his rich cousin possesses, now finds this rich cousin barred entry and his creditors pressing. A person whose parent is resident abroad and sick unto death, is denied the chance of fetching him home to be nursed. The examples are offered quite factually and with no reference to the children's real personal experience nor any prevailing political views on immigration, nor did the teacher invite such observations.

The teacher then invited the children to set up a meeting place to which they as villagers subsequently repaired to await the arrival of the messenger and the announcement of the new law. The teacher had put on a leather coat and arrived as the messenger among the chattering villagers who stood up at his entry. A formal greeting was made and the new edict announced and questions invited. These began politely and sought further clarification of the position. Anger however mounted at the apparent implacable position that prevented exceptional cases or would not admit any compassionate pleading. Some examples of deprivation discussed earlier emerged, but mostly there were new injustices cited and all reached a climax in the passionate cry of a boy, 'Why do you do this? Why do you come here every year and give us another law?' The class wholly united by this outburst went on to cite the uselessness of most of what had been ordained, the repressive constraint of the President's laws and how they believed that a good country and a good government needed few laws not many. The messenger at this point said that debate was not part of his brief but invited the villagers to make representations if they so wished and departed to spread the news to other communities.

The villagers, with the teacher now among them as fellow villager, argued their line of action; emissaries with a letter from the village to the President replaced early demands for violence and civil disobedience, though these measures were to be held in reserve if all attempts at mediation were rejected. The emissaries were chosen and the meeting dispersed.

There is so much to say about the making of that play it is difficult to know where to start. Perhaps the most appropriate observation to begin with would be the teacher/pupil relationship and what were their mutual expectations.

The teacher's assumption entertained no doubt that such creative work was within the capability of the class. The class enjoyed that total confidence of their teacher. Evidence of this mutual trust is in the initial open invitation of the teacher and in a use of language that did not undersell the intelligence of the class. Should a word or sentence be misunderstood the children would say so and the teacher rephrase it. The topic for discussion was a worthy one and did not regard the class as retarded or of limited ability. Finally, and it was characteristic of all the teaching and learning of this class, the questions were genuine and evoked genuine replies.

It would be easy to say that to proceed thus is to make over-generous assumptions and that the class can make a convincing show of understanding without actually doing so. In the drama, however, such a pretence is immediately discernible because the ideas discussed are coined into concrete acts and misunderstanding immediately shows. For example, on one occasion a class in the same multiracial school was preparing to make a play about the ravages of a severe flood. An obvious gap in understanding of the concept of a flood appeared when in a role playing exchange a child denied having seen the flood because as he said, 'I was looking the other way'!

Language in the multicultural classroom

As for all children, there exists in the multicultural classroom opportunity for practising language in various registers both formal and informal. Rarely does it happen that the language demands of the chosen role defeat the player though occasionally there may occur some striking anachronisms. The teacher's function in setting the situational definition in language is obviously vital here. And in such a classroom the teacher has the advantage of working with children who are acutely conscious of language for, as often as not, they serve as interpreters for non-English speaking parents or grandparents. Often teachers of such classes assume that the children suffer irreparable disadvantage in language acquisition whereas, in fact, they are much more acutely aware than their indigenous peers. Their facility appears when the demands being made are such that the child can cope with and especially where being right or wrong is not a predetermined condition. In this activity all contributions are welcomed and given equal consideration and it is the teacher's task to come to terms with what the child is trying to express.

Such a sympathy exercised at all times, not merely in drama activities, increases the bond of friendship and respect between teacher and class. In this example the class verbally attacked the teacher as messenger and bitterly opposed all that he represented as emissary of a repressive regime. The meeting was fast and furious with the sort of verbal exchanges with which we are familiar from the hustings. The teacher was genuinely at risk within the secure confines of the invention, so was the class. This mutual step into the dark tightens the bonds of trust and affection between them and affects their relationships at all times.

Indeed, were the teacher to attempt such familiarity only when playmaking, the result would be disastrous. Especially with children whose parents often have a concept of school as authoritarian establishment and who transmit such an expectation, occasional leniency would be greeted by the children as an invitation to licence.

Finally, in this consideration of relationships, it is important that the child appreciates the teacher as a facilitator of learning but does not expect omniscience. Learning must involve everyone in the classroom including the teacher so that the pupils' self-concept may be enhanced and discovery be a genuine delight. Such intimacy encourages honest exchange of opinion and the reappraisal of social values referred to before.

The exchange of cultural values
A vital factor that must not be overlooked is the exchange of experience of different cultural norms and values that can occur through drama in the multicultural classroom. Such an exchange is exemplified graphically in 'The President's New Law'.

It is essential that it is understood that apart from the interest of the teacher in the whys rather than the hows of lawbreaking, all of his subsequent contributions related to form and not content. This was supplied by the children and clarified by questioning by the teacher in his attempt to come to terms with what the children were trying to conceive. This caveat is necessary not only to counter possible charges of political bias and even indoctrination, but, more important, to appreciate the core concern, the secondary symbolism of the play.

By an overwhelming majority the class chose to exemplify deliberated lawbreaking in a play about Immigration. No one even mentioned the word nor drew parallels from nearer home to make the play a political satire. However, it is remarkable that of all the laws they might have chosen or did consider, this was the one they adopted and although the categorisation of a set of ideas under Lawbreakers was likely to produce a civic theme, nevertheless many other ideas would have been easier to enact. The struggle for the appropriate form was part of the creative achievement and was no easy task. Both teacher and class had to struggle together and the teacher in particular had to retain confidence and not override the class intention because at first sight it seemed unworkable.

Given the minority community's insecurity partly occasioned by Government statements on Entry Regulations, a teacher of different ethnic origin might easily appreciate the significance of the children's choice of theme. What was so revealing and so moving was the expression in dramatic form of what anguish accompanies the denial of the concept of extended families. Where the western pattern in the present century has been towards the nuclear family – father, mother and 2.5 children – and where the enforced mobility that unemployment necessitates has reduced extended family ties, it is difficult for Europeans to appreciate the role of uncles, aunts, grandparents, 'rich cousins'. Furthermore the property owning democracy or the provision of council owned property has contributed to this cultural phenomenon and especially with separate provision for the old.

Whether one pattern or the other is better is irrelevant, we are merely citing the different practices to highlight a problem of misunderstanding within a multicultural society. Certainly the teacher in this instance was brought to a heightened awareness of concerns that he would not otherwise have felt, though perhaps intellectually entertained.

This was not the learning experience of the majority of the children but for them there was an awareness of the civic process in a way that excited interest and provoked discussion and opinion. Whether attitudes were changed would be hard to say as no formal testing was undertaken. But then it is controversial to consider whether learning can, or should be, exhaustively measured.

This play was conducted entirely in English but in the multicultural classroom it is important that respect should be shown to whichever is the child's mother tongue. The over-emphasis upon the majority language can not only appear to denigrate other tongues but constantly reinforce a child's sense of failure and inferiority. It is difficult, though, to conduct classes in many languages where the content is principally abstract and where reliance upon verbal exchange is paramount. In the drama, being a low level of abstraction and concrete in its representation, this difficulty does not exist.

Mention was made earlier about the concept of flood. A play from this idea was made, again involving the nine to ten age group in the same multiracial primary school. The exploration began with no obvious intention of playmaking; the teacher and the class discussing a television news report of a flood disaster in India. The question arose of the filming of people dying of hunger and whether the operation was morally justifiable. If a camera crew could get there, why not food supplies? Would the world's conscience be stirred to the urgency of the need for relief by the showing of their plight on television? Different attitudes were voiced but all had been affected by the pitiful scenes they had so recently witnessed.

The teacher saw the potential in the situation and invited the class to become such a stricken village while he would be a visiting official come to make some assessment of the community's needs. It was suggested that family groups could be formed and this the class did, constructing the most amazing costumes from a box of odd lengths of materials. Three children were not absorbed into any group and remained unhappy and rejected. The teacher, without thinking, said that one could be his interpreter and the others secretaries. The four then left the room which they expected to enter again as the village of the flood victims. From outside the door a fearful noise within could be heard, subsequently discovered to be the class experiencing the holocaust, but it soon lapsed into relative quiet. When the team entered it was to see a sorry sight: people in tattered rags, mute with dejection or rocking slowly and moaning quietly. The official greeted them with, 'Good afternoon. We have been sent by the Government to learn what things are needed for your comfort and relief.' No one responded, even to the extent of paying any attention whatsoever to what had been said. The teacher felt a sudden sense of isolation and anxiety for his presence in the classroom seemed not only superfluous but the class was not even acknowledging his existence. He might have reverted to teacher role in defence and called the class together for a new briefing. Trusting in the sense of commitment of the class, however, he sought in his mind for an explanation. Then it was so obvious, the children did not respond to his official and rather pompous greeting because they did not understand the language!

The official turned to the interpreter and asked her to translate. Here the teacher expected the child to use English as though it were the foreign tongue and nearly fell over when the interpreter spoke to the village in Gujarati. At once there was a response with groups chattering together and passing on the message in language totally incomprehensible to the official, and indeed to the teacher taking that role. He was forced to wait for everything he said to be translated and to seek interpretation of whatever was offered by the villagers. In fact he discovered that a member of one family did speak English, 'Bit, little bit.' A mixture of tongues were then used though apart from that contribution in English there was very little else offered by the villagers except in their own tongues, Bengali and Urdu included. Slowly, painfully slowly, he learnt of their plight, a dead father, a lost husband or wife, and destruction of houses and livestock. The village elder, a doubled up old gentleman but sharp as a tack, acted as intermediary between the interpreter and the village families. Long debate was held over whether plates were needed or pots; the official seemed to insist on everything being written down by his secretaries. Delay and frustration increasingly affected the villagers whose anger spilled out when they discovered that the official was returning, leaving them empty handed, and with more days of hunger and despair before the promised relief would come. The official withdrew, alarmed at the anger and unable to mediate or even explain, shepherding his small retinue.

The class had felt perhaps a bit more the plight of the homeless and bereft, not only in their misery but also in their anger and frustration. Perhaps also they learned some of the problems for relief teams or agents attempting to help. The teacher experienced, as never before, the helplessness and isolation of speaking the minority language and not the majority. The sense of the rhythm of another people and their necessity to keep all informed, for theirs was a genuine community involvement, was overwhelmingly apparent to him also.

In the real class situation the teacher suffered almost complete role-reversal. He not only appeared ignorant, but was so, when he could not speak the language. He relied entirely upon trusting the children not to exploit the situation in any mischievous or malicious way, and was obliged to be led by them. In fact the class were all English speakers, some native, white, Midland-born children, but all had been involved – boys as mothers and babies as well as fathers and grandfathers. The exchange of leadership from class to teacher and back was the stuff of which true Education should be. The deficient one appeared to be the English speaker; the teacher had appeared as perplexed and much slower than his pupils sometimes did when faced with problems of language.

Another, and very different example of Drama in the multicultural classroom took place in a multiracial class of adolescent girls and boys excluded from secondary schools, again in a Midland city. The class was not big, probably some twelve or so pupils, but lively, quick tempered, immediately aggressive but intelligent and articulate. Their first response to doing Drama was with cries of immense derision. Finding that it involved an interesting strategic tussle they joined in quite happily. Especially they enjoyed making their own plays and would use the teacher if short of essential characters. The plays had elaborate plots which were agreed and very often adhered to – a triumph with these disruptive pupils. Very often they were angry plays involving shouting and sometimes violence but the shouting was simulated anger and the violence rarely malevolent. In fact on the whole the plays were good natured, outwardly comic but often representing hard and inconsistent relationships.

The balance of black children and white swung increasingly towards the former as their numbers in the secondary schools grew, and their obvious dissatisfaction with their education became more manifest. Their tolerance thresholds were low, their concentration span short and above all they carried a deep resentment of teachers. These qualities were shared by all, including a few Asian teenage girls, and were apt to explode at almost any time. Acts of spiteful agression were enacted almost all the time and it was the teacher's exhausting task to practise a continual shuttle diplomacy.

The social health of the class then was not good and the particular example we are to examine was culled from a television series about black and white neighbours. The programme had excited debate about whether it beneficially aired racial intolerence or whether in fact it reinforced predjudice. In the classroom it provided an opportunity for the black children to work together, leaving the white children and Asians to the other group. Perhaps an object of the series and certainly a feature of this play was that for all their apparent difference the families shared similar characteristics which, as they gradually revealed themselves, left the families grudgingly surprised.

The similar characteristic in this case resided in a teenage view of home. The mothers, friends and confidantes in both households were drudges, the fathers or elder brothers, unfeeling and loud. In the white household the father veered between an indulgent bonhommie and bouts of spiteful petulance that expressed itself in shouting at the non-offending children. His view of his neighbours was a racialist stereotype complaining of their smell, their dishonesty and objecting to his wife going next door.

The Black neighbours found the Whites dishonest and smelly and always ready to borrow groceries but seldom to return them. The men sat around in the kitchen playing interminable games of cards conducted against an equally unceasing flow of near unintelligible Caribbean dialect. For those who were able to follow, it was a fairly racy conversation but always sufficiently intelligible to allow the play about a mistaken supposition of theft by the Whites from the Blacks, to proceed. Although apparently divided the class worked as one, carefully planting cues to each other and enjoying their joint creation. The plot in this instance was very simple and ended conclusively, the characters were pasteboard and the attitudes predictable and apparently unchanged. How then would one justify the exercise and what lessons does it have for the teacher in the normal multicultural classroom?

As Dr Johnson observed about the dog walking on its hind legs, it was less surprising that it did not perform well, but more remarkable that it happened at all. So with this play which relied upon consensus, a willing suspension of belief, generosity in inter-personal relationships and a commitment that would see the class intention realised. All these qualities that characterise the socially healthy group were rarely normally present for this class. Their tolerance in the play situation survived encounters that otherwise would have resulted in violence and class chaos. Again, that the teacher was prepared to be allotted a minor role which invited derision but which was a vital element in the play, was a step towards better pupil/teacher relationships. Also the teacher did not impose his own invention but was prepared to share in communal, honest criticism. The class had adopted a familiar model but discovered that the form was in suspense, a significant present, maintained by visible actions and reactions. This latter point the children never articulated as a theory, but certainly realised in the playing.

The Black children especially, used the occasion to project the most striking and provocative image of themselves both visually and verbally. One can well imagine such a display, like the booted skinhead White, threatening the teacher's authority and leading to the eventual suspension they had all incurred. In this setting, though, it proved an amusing, appropriately selected portrayal that, far from threatening, actually supported the class activity and the teacher's part in it. These children, both Whites and Blacks, as adolescents often will, had tried out a role that, taken too seriously by adults, could evoke a resentful and determined defence of something they would otherwise concede quite willingly.

Perhaps we should end where we began and review not only the role of drama in the multicultural classroom but that very term itself, bearing in mind that the monoracial classroom is still part of a wider ethnically mixed society as a whole.

Language acquisition

There are obvious advantages to be gained by using drama as an aid to language acquisition. This needs qualifying, for to give the same meaning to this activity as to all else we have described would be nonsense. Here one merely means a mimetic activity that indicates already in its concrete representation, the meaning of the unfamiliar language.

I once had a group of students who were training to teach French and we wanted to try out some 'dramatic' techniques to assist the work. I had little experience of language teaching, other than English, though my Latin classes of many years ago were constantly trying to make the learning spring from the concrete and practical. Anyway we went to that same multiracial primary school where none of the children spoke French. They were not at that time familiar with me and so some ten or eleven strangers appeared in the class. I greeted them in French and continued to say in the language how pleased we were that they had agreed to help us. The children looked blank and uneasy for I seemed to have some expectation of them they could not meet. I stopped and sought from them in English that they were French speakers as I had been told. 'No' they wailed with eyes large at the obvious mistake that had occurred. I turned to the students and explained the situation in French at which they clicked their tongues and showed annoyance. I asked the children's guidance; it was too late to go elsewhere, would they help us to learn how to teach French? This we would measure by if at the end of the hour these children could speak a little of the language. They assented and my students who spoke no English throughout the visit moved in to work with groups of three or four children. They taught each child a sentence or phrase using only a vital mimetic communication- 'Comment allez-vous?' 'Je bois du café', etc. The children were helped first to understand the sentence and then to reproduce it. All were introduced to, 'Étes vous Francais?' and 'Oui' and 'Non'. The sentences had been chosen so that they could have some continued conversational quality, the student supplying the majority of the talk but the child responding to his particular piece.

The class was brought together and was asked whether anyone could think of an example of where as non-speakers of a language they might need to appear as natives of that foreign country. We knew the children had discussed with their teacher a recent television film about the Dutch Resistance and they suggested, as we supposed they might, escaping prisoners. So we set up the scene; a French café with a French girl as the Patron, with apron and expansive greeting, the desks became tables around which sat some students speaking the language, with the prisoners practising their phrase just in case. Suddenly the door opened and two helmeted leather coated soldiers with guns appeared and said in English, 'We are looking for escaped prisoners, are they here?' The patron in French denied having seen them but the soldiers remained unconvinced, surveying the café crowd whose chattering had now resumed after the awesome silence of the soldiers' entry. In order to test whether these were genuine natives the soldiers dropped on various people. 'Étes-vous Francais?' they would demand and always came the confident reply, 'Oui Monsieur'. It seemed too easy though, and the soldiers remained obviously suspicious. Then, suddenly, they beckoned a large boy, 'Venez-ici'. He got up and came forward. 'He's not French' said one soldier to the other, 'let's really test him'. Swinging round they fired the question, 'Quelle heure est-il?', 'Deux heures et demi' he replied – being *his* phrase as the students well knew – 'He must be French' the soldier said with obvious disappointment, then 'Asseyez-vous' with a dismissive wave of the hand. The people at the tables breathed again, the boy as he returned, and with his back to the soldiers, winked at his fellow prisoners and furtively showed a thumbs up in triumph. The soldiers having glared again at the assembly went out of the door, and the whole class expressed its relief, triumph and prowess.

This intensely theatrical episode was fun and absorbed the class entirely. I do not know whether it was an accepted language teaching technique but the students took from it what they saw as appropriate and I was told successfully used 'a drama approach' in subsequent class teaching practice. The children were amazed at how enjoyable the experience had been as older brothers and sisters at secondary school had told them of how boring was learning a foreign language. Certainly a year later some of them would still greet me with the phrase they had learned.

The exercise might seem elaborate and it was, for it was for the benefit of the students more than the children. It was intended to demonstrate that you do not teach a language in particular, without a great deal of projecting of one's self into the operation. The teacher has to establish the language from the relationship, whereas so often it is from the exchanges in language that we build interpersonal relationships. This latter process is often slow and cautious with oneself being revealed little by little. To teach a language, perhaps even the mother tongue, the teacher must step into the dark, trusting to the generosity of the learners.

It is this attempt to enact the language that allows us to talk of using 'Drama' to teach a language. In fact to expect a foreign language flow for real drama we all remember from our own experience, if only of holidays abroad, is another matter entirely. It helps though when we are among real people speaking the language to some purpose. The simulation of the shop or the doctor's waiting room in the classroom can be rather daunting because one never seems to have enough command to be easy in role.

The opportunity that drama provides for trying differing modes of language is as valuable in the multicultural classroom as any other. Especially as the class has a knowledge of the invented scenario there is an appreciation of the rules and tactics of the drama game that is in progress.

There is concern expressed by Her Majesty's Inspectors in the report 'Aspects of the Secondary Curriculum' that all children should be made aware of being part of a multicultural society. The need is perhaps greater they feel in those areas where ethnic minority groups are not encountered than in the urban conurbations with their multiracial populations. The sentiment is worthy but drama in such circumstances is likely to use the setting of a multicultural situation in order to explore a much more universal concept - exploitation, discrimination, predjudice, etc. We would hope to increase the class awareness not of the characteristics of Sikhs, Jamaicans, Vietnamese, Puerto Ricans but of their right to be encountered as people like ourselves. In the rural areas what is the attitude towards gypsies, in the North the attitude towards Southerners, and in the South the attitude towards everywhere else?

We need to encourage a preparedness to examine other ways and other convictions, not to abandon our own necessarily, but to learn to share our lives more generously with our fellows whatever their persuasion.

Finally, this chapter does not seek to encourage its readers to ignore that there are differences in classes, especially those with members of different ethnic groups. Rather it supports the view of the multicultural classroom as rich with resources from which all can benefit. The different issues and practices are an immense stimulus to learning that grows from discovery rather than instruction only. The teacher never knows what wonders lie around the next corner as for example when in a play about Gossip set in a local store a little girl playing a battered mother-in-law showed her scarred head to the shopkeeper, and her bruised leg and concluded vehemently, 'And he (her son-in-law) gave me three black eyes'!

Summary
Drama is an aid to language acquisition in the multicultural classroom but the chapter argues the greater importance of cultural understanding. The concept of a pluralist society is perhaps a little more understood through the operation of the Drama Game with its emphasis upon sharing. Especially important is the understanding gained by the teacher through an appreciation of the secondary symbolism expressed through the play.

7

Drama as a Teaching Aid

Drama, unlike other parts of the curriculum, suffers from the speculation that it does not deserve to be considered as a separate subject. Wisely the DES Drama Survey contended that already too much time and energy had been spent disputing this question, and the question of whether Drama should be taught only by specialists. But any consideration of how drama relates to the curriculum as a whole must grasp this nettle once again.

The arguments that recommend separate departments of drama to gain advantage for the subject in the school are well rehearsed, but no less important for that reason. Certainly the continued need to secure adequate provision both of physical facilities and, much more, fair distribution of contact through the whole age range, is critical. But if we wish to avoid mere factionalism, we must examine what is drama's unique contribution and justify its inclusion on those grounds. For then we shall need no other.

Much of this justification has already been suggested, particularly in the previous chapter, where the dramatic process was carefully laid out in graphic detail. Perhaps what still remains to be covered is a fuller study of the Inquiry stage in relation to drama and other subjects, and how practical questions of space and numbers affect the work.

The emergence of drama as an examinable subject at GCE and CSE has tended to confirm the mistaken impression that what distinguishes drama as a subject are theatre skills and the history of theatre and dramatic literature. But though this gives a body of examinable fact, to study drama thus is to deny the essential discipline through which experience is organised. For drama is doing, as Aristotle wrote, 'an imitation of an action' – a model of an encounter. Therefore any studies in drama should radiate from the process itself, elaborations on the rules and strategies of the Drama Game. So, for example, might we study the skill of ball control, but it would be meaningful only in so far as it extended our understanding of the game of football. In drama all should tend to a greater understanding of the concept of drama both aesthetically and socially. In this way we appreciate how the drama works but also why it is necessary to man's being, a greatly neglected consideration at this time.

The Education Pamphlet No. 57, 'Towards the Middle School' suggests that with the middle school child it is not our aim to produce specialists but to help them to understand more about their world and to enjoy their lives. This is more likely to happen, it contends, from a 'school learning which is geared to an all-round study of problems.'[1] Furthermore the solutions of such 'day to day problems and the pursuit of interests often makes demands on knowledge and skills associated with several subject disciplines.' Above all, it stresses, 'children must always be encouraged to seek for meaning, for pattern and interconnections.'[2]

This seeking for meaning and pattern may be achieved by operating different disciplines separately or in concert and may be expressed also in many different ways. Often we stress reading and writing to the exclusion of other experiences. Modern maths has assisted many to a greater insight into the way that subject examines such relationships as size and distance and the patterns of shapes. In English a movement towards oracy has greatly stimulated the study of the written word. Science, too, though always including a measure of experiment for older children, has more recently extended to younger children this opportunity for genuine discovery. Similarly the use of drama in the class promotes an active search for meaning by living through the stress of people's lives.

That drama deals in such problems of human relationships is by now, I hope, well established. It does not, however, attempt to offer solutions but examines the dilemma from many points of view with more than just the intellect. The range of its inquiry is obviously as immense as the things men say and do to each other. The extent to which perception is gained from the study will depend upon the maturity of the players.

To study the subject itself will be to attempt to perfect the skills the game of drama demands, and to become more acutely aware of the symbolic power of speech and gesture. In addition, when communicating insights through the form of the theatre, extra-verbal stimuli such as light and sound, setting and costume, assist to convey a 'total and external code of values and norms of conduct from which the speech and action of the play is drawn' (70). This whole realm of experience will be examined more fully in the next chapter.

Drama as a tool

Our major concern at present is with the drama as a tool, as a means of organising experience gained casually in the traffic of everyday life, or selectively through subject study. And to conduct such inquiry requires a teacher conversant with the process of drama and the application of its resources to the classroom situation. Above all the teacher must possess an ability to read the class, to appreciate its needs and then how to satisfy these needs using drama, if appropriate. Also, needs that drama may satisfy are those of concrete experience as a base for thinking, the concrete operational process. But inevitably it will distort, because the criteria employed are derived from a subjective interpretation of the material. Therefore it must be realised that the dramatic process cannot stand instead of the other study, history, geography, etc. It serves, as suggested earlier, as a means of exploring material to gain insight into social implications, or to communicate our understanding of the material through the dramatic form.

It is clear, then, that it is vitally important to the success of the work, that the teacher is aware at the outset, at the Inquiry, to what end he is using the drama tool; indeed, whether it is appropriate to use the drama at all on that occasion. He will need to know whether he intends his source material to remain dominant throughout, or whether it serves merely as a starting point for a much freer inquiry. Let us look at some brief examples of such decisions taken with children of middle school age.

A class of top juniors has read an abridged version of *Oliver Twist*. The teacher often makes, with the class, free versions of such stories and presents them, using drama and dance with costumes and properties. All such preparation is bound into the curriculum so that it is a part of the learning and not an extra chore. Whether the work follows the usual pattern now depends upon a host of things; whether the work appeals to the class, what other pressures may be upon them or upon the teacher, whether or not a rest from the inevitable pressures of performance might not be good for all concerned. In her lessons this teacher will use different approaches, but most are aimed at consolidating the children's memory and understanding of the events of the story. They dramatise the novel's plot, though their hand in the selection of events and how they are shown, supplies a purpose, not always apparent in such exercises. On this occasion the class put together their selected scenes, the Workhouse that uses a machine sequence, a London street with a chorus of street cries, the handkerchief game in Fagin's den as a piece of dance. It is generally well undertaken, each group choosing to present which episode takes its fancy. The 'performances' show that the class has retained, absorbed and reproduced not only bits of original dialogue but has also translated some literary effects into a dramatic form.

The class has moved through the period of Inquiry gaining a greater perception of the relationships implicit in the text, through playing them. And here the lesson stops, for there is no intention of using the events of the novel to illustrate contemporary life and its dilemmas. The original source material has remained largely unchanged throughout, different only in that it has been animated.

Before the class is dismissed the pupils reflect upon their achievement. They are asked which of the pieces they most enjoyed watching, why they thought it superior to the others, and had it been a play in its own right, what would it have been called. The questions are designed to allow the class to express, though not dramatically, the perceived relationships. As it happens, the favourite is the episode in Fagin's den when Oliver is introduced to picking pockets by the playing of an apparently innocent game. The children decide that were it a play it might be called *The Loss of Innocence*, a melodramatic title but perfectly expressing the core, the gestus as Brecht calls it, of the scene; the game. The class, clear about the issues, have no difficulty suggesting modern equivalents, all of which could supply material for future dramatic work. For, in their reflection they have embarked upon a new Inquiry, though shortage of time will not allow them to pursue it further on this occasion. Were they to do so then they would depart from the original source material as it would have served its purpose as a stimulus, as subject matter for the Inquiry. The teacher's aim in that case would not have been primarily revisory but to provide a creative departure from the original. And such a course of action would not have been more or less better than the other, only more appropriate, in his opinion.

Whichever way is chosen, in each case the source material provides the rules of the drama game that emerges from it. Where that material is the more important feature of the work, then the game abides by the rules it sets. Where it is intended only as a starting place, its content may be changed, its rules altered by the players' consensus. For example, we may see the same basic exploitation of people in these two extracts, one from the Factories of the Nineteenth Centry and the other from the Eighteenth Century Slave-Trade. However, the first sets out a precise and detailed scenario for a dramatic exploration, while the second might be transposed into our own time where there is still little room for the old.

First: 'The door of the lodge will be closed ten minutes after the engine starts every morning, and no weaver will afterwards be admitted till breakfast-time. Any weaver who may be absent during that time shall forfeit three-pence per loom.

On one occasion we counted *ninety-five* persons that were thus locked out at half-past five o'clock in the morning. The way in which this method of genteel robbery was accomplished, was by putting the clocks half an hour forward – that is, it was fifteen minutes later than the public clocks of the town in the evening and fifteen minutes forwarder in the morning. These ninety-five persons were fined three-pence each...'[3]

Second: 'Fryday 1st December... At daylight saw the longboat in shoar. She came on board at 8, brought with her 4 slaves, 2 fine boys and an old man and woman not worth their room which, if possible, I must dispose of again.'[4]

In the first example not a word can be ignored; it reflects a merciless authority which was eventually to be eroded. To attempt to perceive insights into the age, it is necessary to be alert to every clue, every pointer, for nothing is irrelevant. But the second is somewhat different. True, the passage is taken from the diary of a slave trader and reflects the treatment of his human cargoes as non-people. But this particular piece has as its focus the additional wretchedness of old age, uselessness and redundancy. The plight of slaves is perhaps difficult for all of us to understand, but the slavery to old age is more familiar and all too relevant.

Increasingly in books intended for drama teachers there is greater use being made of source material that might have been regarded at one time as being the province of another subject. Also the history book or the text from social or environmental studies will recommend that drama be employed to achieve a greater sympathy with the subject under review. So in the series by Martin and Vallins, or Hodgson and Richards, and in David Kemp's *A Different Drummer* (24) it is possible to find sensitively selected extracts as source material for the Inquiry. But the teacher should be clear about how the material is to be used. He must be able to see how the extract is illustrative of what concerns the class.

With such awareness the teacher will come to rely, perhaps, more on his own discoveries or upon those of the class. And there is an immensely rich source of potential material for drama all around us, in letters to newspapers and magazines, in labels on cans, in advertisements and horoscopes, in the whole realm of human activity that is recorded in word, in sound and in pictures.

There is, for example, the advertisement that attempts to persuade one to 'Send a Can'. The product is a push-button can of deodorant which the firm suggests is more effective 'than the one your friend is using'. They suggest that if one sends a dollar they will send the can, 'in a plain brown wrapper', and conclude that the friend 'will never know who to thank'! The drama reveals the insensitivity of a would-be sender and the painful embarrassment of the recipient. Equally the bland words of a horoscope that warns 'an unexpected letter may lead to family problems' becomes a nightmare when made a reality with all the responsibility of human relationships.

Even such familiar warnings as 'Keep off the Grass' can provide a useful starting point for exploring social attitudes, and so can the exhortation of 'Make hay while the sun shines'. David Kemp draws attention to the words of 'Eleanor Rigby' and how they offer such a starting point, and so do the lyrics of many popular songs like 'If you can't please everyone, you'd better please yourself', 'How can people be so heartless? How can they ignore their friends?', and 'I can't get no satisfaction'.

The personal column of a newspaper can set a problem of invention with a cryptic message: 'Snowball. Same place. 24th. Sam', as can a telegram, like this, 'George come Home. Mother Worse. Vi'. And as baffling can be the copy when divorced from the picture of an advertisement – 'You can always say it's the wife's', 'Put yourself in our shoes', 'Bittermen – Join them!'.

These examples serve only to show the range of sources, and they barely start such a list. Even more difficult would be to outline how they ought to be treated. It is sufficient to take any one of them and simply regard it as a play for, say, four people. For in this way the players use the drama to exemplify the thought that lies behind the original statement and in so doing may reveal the truth or falsity of the attitude. And this is the social function of the art, as we recognise in such titles as, *The Way of the World, The Rules of the Game, Happy Days, The Hero Rises Up*. Sometimes explicit from the start, at other times concealed, the play examines a set of social beliefs against the background of the lives of a set of fictitious people. We, with our experience of living, put ourselves in the shoes of these people who are encountering problems which, though they may be extreme, are not unfamiliar to us.

The numbers that are engaged upon a play will depend upon many considerations. Always we will recognise that drama is a group activity, sometimes involving only two, sometimes 'a cast of thousands'. But we will be concerned, as teachers of drama, that the organisation of the class is governed by what we know of how it is accustomed to work, or how the pupils work best. But then, again, we must be sure that the size of the group is related to the nature of the task, and that may be to find a problem for twenty-four people living in modern times. If, however, a class is not used to working in such numbers the teacher will need to define the game and its rules and strategies very clearly until the class is more confident. Above all the room in which one has to work will prove an inescapable factor in determining how numbers involved in the drama game are distributed.

Clearly the circumstances of a classroom are very different from those of a hall or drama studio. The question of disturbing other classes is a real one and is more inhibiting than lack of space to move about freely. And there is nothing that will remove the problem of noise that is caused by a number of people all talking at the same time. Just planning talk can attain an alarming volume as all teachers, not only those of drama, well know. Indeed, much of the work that purports to be drama is characterised by the same fear of the class being noisy, which results in a preponderance of mime and of teacher-controlled exercises. But there is a difference between talking to some purpose and the sort of uncontrolled hysteria that sometimes accompanies so-called drama lessons. Indeed, to provide room for such licence seems to have become accepted perhaps, again, in the profaned name of 'self-expression'. Which is not to say that it is preferable for all concerned that dramatic activity should be able to be noisy if the invention requires it or that it should be enabled to enjoy freedom of space. But it is wrong to suggest, as some manuals do, that drama is impossible without such facilities. It is simply that the task must be appropriate to the physical surroundings, so that 'The Bank Robbery' will consist of the human problems confronting the players, not the physical. For example, there is all the essence of the dramatic process in two or three people going over a map of the layout of a building or a neighbourhood, especially if one of them fears another conviction, having spent too much of his life in prison already, while another, the stronger, has no police record. Brian Way's *Development Through Drama* (47) in the chapter on 'Speaking' is particularly effective in the way that it provides, in its suggestions, the dramatic quality of conflict of interest. Without this ingredient it does not matter where the work takes place, it will lack the feature that above all characterises the exchanges as dramatic, the driving momentum of the drama game.

The process is more than oracy, more than the exercise of spoken English. It is the active playing of the drama game by players, in role, who create a sense of a living present from material already known. So the players know that one of them, and which one, will make difficulties over the plans, but as characters they do not know for it will emerge from a series of moves. Where they are going as players, they know; how they get there will depend upon the way they play the game and that can never be the same way twice.

A history teacher was considering the social history of the eighteenth century with a class of ten-year-olds. Among other things she had introduced costume illustrations which remained displayed on the wall. At one point she distributed photocopies of accounts of highway robberies with their reward details, all having occurred within the vicinity of where the school now stood. Each pair of children had a description which they read and then one of them was to claim the reward by giving information about the crime. The sergeant's cross-examination of the informant elicited details about dress and many other aspects of the life of the times that the children were unaware that they knew. But the game depended upon the maintenance of the sense of really having been at the scene using a combination of facts from the report and anything else that might have been learned during the study. And there was a competitive sense in which one player would try to catch out the other, both as players and as characters when they reward was at stake.

The use of the drama in this way lasted maybe for ten minutes, perhaps a little longer. No one moved from his seat, and the noise was never excessive though nearly forty children were talking at more or less the same time. The teacher did not ask the pairs to perform though they did report on what sort of information had arisen during the conversation. The class, used to using drama to explore and express, regarded the task with no more surprise than if they had been invited to write about the incident. They clearly enjoyed the experience but did not over-enthuse or complain about resuming a more traditional way of learning.

For the teacher there was an indication of the level at which the work was being experienced, how far the class was able to conceive of life in another age, and whether the details of the life of the times made the crime essentially different from a similar incident today. Such questions might lead on to a consideration of crime and punishment as a whole and what reforms have led to our present system, which is by no means faultless.

Ten minutes, then, of effective use of drama in a classroom, and heavily teacher-centred in its definition. Yet that short time was perhaps worth more than many hours of 'reeling and writhing' in the hall to musically-accompanied themes, posing as freely chosen but equally imposed by the teacher. For the first teacher knew what the process of drama involved and why she felt that it was appropriate at this time. The task was clear to the class and involved them in exercising skills of social interaction that they possess in abundance and use almost continually. The second experience, however, can often amount to no more than a set of misunderstood routines that initially attract because they appear as not requiring effort of mind or great bodily discipline. Why the work is being carried forward is not clear to the children nor often to the teacher either, and the result can be at worst a riot.

The non-specialist may see how he might use the game of drama to assist the organisation of the experience of his subject, a genuine inter-disciplinary method. It remains for us in the succeeding chapters to examine the relationship of the drama game to theatre and dramatic literature and, briefly, its place in the life of the community.

Summary

The relationship of drama to other subjects is shown to lie in its employment as a means of organising experience. With the aid of the model introduced in the previous chapter, advice is given for the use of drama in English, History and other-subjects. Above all the drama is studied in this chapter as being an addition to the non-specialist drama teacher's classroom technique.

Notes

1 DES (54) page 12
2 DES (54) page 12
   2a BURNS (70) page 83
3 PIKE (71) page 62
4 NEWTON page 71

Further Reading

Hodgson and Richards (17)   Parry (35)
Kemp (24)   Cook (6)
Moffatt (32)   Fines and Verier (9)

The selection above represents a number of manuals representing sound structured approaches to drama teaching. Cook (6) was one of the earliest advocates of the use of drama. Hodgson and Richardson (18) and Kemp (24) especially make use of a wide variety of popular source material.

8

Drama, Dramatic Literature and Theatre

A major setback to the understanding of teaching drama has been the barrier that has been erected between drama and both dramatic literature and the theatre. This opposition arose from the justifiable condemnation of the then existing concepts of drama teaching in schools. Too often this appeared as adult-centred amateur dramatics with children, or a dreary reading round the class of some incomprehensible text. The former resulted, very often, in an exposure to audiences far too early in the child's life, and in the imposition of actor's skills in circumstances that rendered them mere empty rituals. The latter emphasised the famous rubric of the context question, 'Who said what, to whom and on what occasion?' rather than the more vital question 'Why?' So it was that many felt these mistaken concepts were doing great harm to the child's appreciation of drama and his ability to use it to express his own thoughts and feelings.

Because this thinking coincided with a new interest in the educational and developmental properties of play, with the study of children's art and music, and with experiments in theatre for children, it tended to reject rather than re-examine existing practices. A new definition of drama emerged that excluded both text and presentation in a theatrical form, calling these experiences 'interpretive', as opposed to the 'expressive' function of the drama. The presence of an audience was disallowed as was written material for children to enact. The title 'Improvisation' covered a host of activities, most lacking definition, structure or understanding, but supported by inappropriately borrowed disciplines or partially-digested child psychology. Typical of the confusion was the term 'Polished Improvisation', seemingly a contradiction in terms. In fact it was no more than the application of theatre constraints to a dramatic invention originating from a group. Such apparent inconsistencies not explained by the advocates of the new drama repeatedly confronted puzzled teachers; children *liked* performing, they endlessly made up their own plays and their fellows seemed to be enchanted by them. Increasingly classes asked for 'real plays', and the backward child seemed to draw some sense of security from a not too difficult play script. Sometimes it appeared that the drama teacher, sticking rigidly to dogmatic theories of educational drama, was the person least able to recognise the children's needs, much less accommodate them.

Drama and Performance

Now such behaviour, aberrations in the eyes of some teachers, reveals the child's desire for structure, for a secure starting point. And, though meagre in potential, such plays are enjoyed and used by children who thereby submit themselves to the rules of an invention, as we saw in the dramatic play of the young child. What we are saying, then, is that there is an inclination in children's invention towards the play form as familiarised for them by theatre or television. Inevitably they will aspire to create plays that resemble those that appear to be universally approved as successful – *Softly, Softly, Star Trek, Kung Fu,* etc. These represent, through consensual support, what they regard as 'real' drama, while often what the teacher recommends seems pointless and artificial in comparison.

Nor should we be contemptuous of this view or the imitations that the children present, for drama teaching is to blame if they lack understanding or sensibility. It is currently fashionable, when criticising the failure of drama teaching, to cite the stereotypes that emerge from the domestic scenes that children enact – 'mums from detergent advertising...'[1] The charge is that they do not reflect the real life of the participants, but rather their bland acceptance of the TV model as a substitute reality. They do not bother to invent, to honestly create, but are content to settle for what has been given the seal of cheap, popular approval. This view, shot through with dubious value judgements and revealing the teacher's besetting sin of always knowing better, fails to penetrate the more subtle undercurrents of what is actually being played, what it represents. Is this paste-board family breakfast episode merely the usual diatribe against parental authority? Certainly that may appear the theme, but then the children of the family are presented as equally intolerant. Above all, we should notice *how* the piece is being played. What skills of language and non-verbal communication are being employed is what matters, and how the intention of the group is carried through by co-operation and team understanding, though the conclusion be inconsequential. In a similar way we might observe, in a ball game, embryonic individual and group skills that, as teachers, we may encourage and perfect towards a greater enjoyment of the game. And we would not expect to see such a transformation overnight. For we would acknowledge the limitations of physique, of group immaturity and intellect, that will affect their very grasp of the concept of the game. We would encourage the process involved in playing the game, without labouring the constraints that would attend its being played at the highest level. And this is exactly how teaching drama should be considered.

In the first chapter drama is defined as a process involving the creation of a significant present through representing social behaviour in role. We have observed this same process being employed by the young child and the growing child, in the classroom and in the curriculum, and affected by increasing constraints of social consensus and academic purpose. Now in considering the relationship of drama to dramatic literature and theatre, we are extending our recognition of the additional constraints that attend the art of drama. We see the elaboration through the incidence of rules set by a playwright or by the essential dynamics of the interaction of actors and audience in the theatre. The rules are no longer constructed by the players themselves as a framework for an experimental investigation. They now are imposed and exert a discipline that harnesses the creative energy of the actors and leads it towards expressing 'common meanings and common means of communication.'[2]

Though we appreciate this elaboration we should not make the mistake of thinking that the dramatic process changes. It remains the same, the constant interplay that provides momentum and the payoff – the apprehension of destiny. Nor should we allow ourselves to become so intrigued with the intricacies of the constraints – the characteristics of text or the techniques behind the theatre arts – that we overlook the dramatic process itself. For then we no longer learn *through* drama but only *about* drama; a pursuit that is unproductive unless we appreciate the other active commitment. Which is not to say that drama, dramatic literature and theatre are incompatible studies. Indeed not only do we maintain that the dramatic process is essential to them all, but also that drama, as a learning tool, may be applied for greater understanding and appreciation of the other two. In other words, we may organise our experience of these other studies through the drama, making concrete what is abstract or obscure, and relating it to our past experience, thereby creating new knowledge.

The Text
Let us start by looking at the text and how drama can be used to explore and illuminate its implications.

Francis Fergusson in *The Idea of a Theatre* (8), when talking about the actor's training refers to the purpose of improvisation. He stresses that the freedom of the actors' exchanges is always within the structure of the rules of the game. 'When skilled actors improvise a playlet upon an imagined situation, they respond freely to each other's actions and words within it, yet never violate its basic *donnees*.' Such freedom with control he holds as a fundamental training, but stresses that it is not an end in itself, but merely leads to the literature of the drama, just as the performer's technique of the violinist leads to the literature of the violin, where the possibilities of the instrument are explored.[3] The text, then, is the score, and the action the music which can result from sensitive recreation of the original inspiration.

Stanislavski, the great Russian director, warns against too great a preoccupation with the end product rather than the means. In *An Actor Prepares* (45) he says, 'The mistake most actors make is to think about the result instead of about the action that must prepare it. By avoiding action and aiming straight at the result you get a forced product which can lead to nothing but ham acting.'[4] What we mean by 'ham' acting is the performance of 'an inexperienced or ineffective actor', a performance that does not strike us as having 'truth, fullness and integrity of purpose'. This can happen when the player has failed to penetrate the sense of the text, for though 'the texture of language is reaching towards the experiences that Beethoven imitated in patterns of sound – yet it is not music, it cannot be abstracted from its sense.'[5]

When we talk of the 'sense' of the text we do not mean merely its meaning in a cognitive way but also in an affective way. And to respond so requires a 'living through' of the experience that it implied in the language of the text. For there is, hidden in the blueprint that is the text, the design for action. And 'every *action* meets with a *reaction* which in turn intensifies the first. In every play, beside the main action we find its opposite *counteraction*. This is fortunate because its inevitable result is more action. We need that clash of purposes, and all the problems to solve that grow out of them. They cause the activity which is the basis of our art.'[6] Look at the movement in the following exchange;

DAVIES Where are you going, you going out?
ASTON Yes
DAVIES *(seizing the sandals)* Wait a minute then, just a minute.
ASTON What are you doing?
DAVIES *(putting on the sandals)* I better come with you.
ASTON Why?
DAVIES I mean, I better come out with you anyway.
ASTON Why?
DAVIES Well... don't you want me to go out?
ASTON What for?

DAVIES I mean... when you're out. Don't you want me to get out... when
       you're out?
ASTON You don't have to go out.
DAVIES You mean... I can stay here?
ASTON Do what you like. You don't have to come out just because I go
       out.
DAVIES You don't mind me staying here?
ASTON I've got a couple of keys. *(He goes to a box by his bed and finds them.)*
       This door and the front door. *(He hands them to Davies).*
DAVIES Thanks very much, the best of luck.

Pinter, whose writing this is, taken from his play *The Caretaker*,[7] is
quoted as saying that it is not that his characters do not communicate but
that they communicate too well. In this piece the tramp, Davies, feels the
artlessness of Aston and is thrown by it. Cunning, violence and exploitation
he can manage for they are the features of his daily life, but honesty and
gentle trust is unfamiliar and makes him suspicious. The passage reveals
the tramp's growing awareness that Aston is not, apparently, the stronger of
the two of them, a situation he later seeks to exploit.

On the surface the exchange may seem no more than a simple invitation
of Aston's enabling Davies to stay at home. It could even appear to show the
kindness of Aston to a Davies overcome with such unfamiliar hospitality.
And, in a way, it does, but also so much more waits to be revealed. For in the
pauses, in the groping for words, in the very rephrasing of the questions, we
see the strategy of this game of drama. It moves from the tramp's
assumption that he is the weaker party to the final 'the best of luck', the
classic reply of the beggar to someone who has just given alms: less an
acknowledgement of generosity than a triumph.

Now although the situation can be explained in words, it remains an
abstraction, not the concrete, dynamic encounter of two complex people.
To assist this understanding it is vital to play the piece, not merely to stand
and say the words but to experience the movement of thought and feeling.
The process of rehearsal involves just this experience and the director's job
is to 'help the actor see and overcome his own obstacles'.[8] One way is
through the use of exercises and improvisation for within their game rule-
structure the player can achieve genuine spontaneity and freedom to both
see and solve his problems.

Brook in *The Empty Space* (5) describes some of the ways he and his
actors worked when rehearsing plays which were later acclaimed all over
the world as brilliant performances full of insights and superbly relevant in
expression for our own time. He, rightly, warns the reader against trying to

use his recollections as a handbook for, as he says, 'there are no formulas: there are no methods'.[9] The assistance they give is as example not precept. They show how the players may be brought to an awareness of the nature of the game they are playing, what skills are required and how rehearsals and performances are a continuing search for meaning and significance. Especially clear from his examples is the relationship of this more experimental work to the text.

Another book that treats this same illumination of the text by drama is *Improvisation* by John Hodgson and Ernest Richards (18). The authors cover the values contained in the group process of improvisation, working without text and, finally, improvisation towards the text. The book suggests many excellent starting points without being dogmatic or over-ambitious in its claims for drama.

Despite the help that the teacher might derive from such sources as these we have mentioned, there is, nevertheless a dearth of suitable scripted plays for children. It is a great pity that the wealth of excellent material to be found currently in children's literature is mostly confined to prose and poetry. It seems strange that we take for granted the child's ability to appreciate the art of the novelist, a much more abstract form, yet question whether he can enjoy the more concrete experience of the work of the dramatist. Perhaps had we enjoyed drama teaching in schools of comparable skill and understanding as the teaching of literature then there would be a greater demand for good plays for children. As it is, by eschewing written forms and concentrating only on improvisation, we have set back the contribution that could be made by our dramatists to the education of the child.

In these circumstances it is for the teacher to use his good judgement of what is appropriate for the class and its needs. As Dorothy Heathcote says, 'Whether a play is taken from a book or conjured from the child's own experience, depends not upon a teacher's beliefs, but upon the child's needs and abilities'.[10] So that the class is ready, willing and able to attempt in scripts will govern the choice of dramatic activities. And the teacher will use drama as a way of revealing the meaning of the text and, perhaps more importantly, how the game of drama as represented by the text is played. To do this does not require either immensely profound works or very lengthy texts; it is much more important that it is enjoyed for its content and is of a comfortable length. Too often people undertake pages of dialogue in which are contained far too many problems to be solved at one time. The short Pinter extract could occupy a class very easily, for the problems it poses can be related to other settings, the roles reversed or unexpected turns taken in

Summary
The discipline of the drama is related to the study of the text and to the
DRAMA, DRAMATIC LITERATURE AND THEATRE

the action. The non-verbal aspects of the exchange and the lengths of
pauses, all these things are not merely aspects of technique but are genuine
explorations of social communication skills encountered everyday and of
role definition.

Above all, such studies should encourage children to try to write
themselves. Simple scripts that provide the rules of a dramatic exchange
can be based upon much of the ephemeral material that we mentioned
earlier – newspapers, advertisements, letters, etc. The translation of the
literary material into the dramatic mode can occur in improvisation or in
drafting the blueprint for action, the text. Indeed, what is conceived in
action can be refined and disciplined by the constraint of writing the piece
for others to act. It is an elaboration of the rules, an understanding of the
craft of the playwright by actually writing oneself. As long as the task is not
made too difficult by expecting a standard of excellence beyond the child,
then there is no reason why children should not be encouraged both to write
and present their plays.

Theatre
The presentation of dramatic work at any level, whether informally to one's
classmates or in the more formal theatre setting, requires skill. Very often
when teachers criticise the dramatic pieces that children show, it is in terms
of their skills as actors – the audibility, the credibility of the performance.
Yet they do not teach these skills, though they will censure their absence.
Such a paradox, surely not to be found elsewhere in education, arises from
the teacher's lack of understanding of the aims and methods of drama
teaching. For to insist upon what are often dead theatre rituals is to ignore
the more central purposes of the craft of acting.

A well known and highly regarded book *Improvisation for the Theatre* by
Viola Spolin (44), contains over two hundred theatre games, exercises
aimed at encouraging the efficient and sensitive use of communication
techniques. They are very clear in their aims and procedures and always
relate to the problem of showing, which is partly what theatre is about.
Spolin would add that the games not only assist the development of
performers but also of discriminating and knowledgeable audiences. For
they are conducted in the spirit of games playing and show how the
interaction between actor and actor, and actor and audience is strategic.
'When our theatre training can enable the future playwrights, directors and
actors to think through the role of the audience as individuals and as part of
the process called theatre, each one with a right to a thoughtful and personal
experience, is it not possible that a whole new form of theatre presentation

will emerge?'[11] Certainly the author's advice to teachers about how to work with children is wise and helpful.

There are many books that describe how the class may construct relatively cheap and effective properties and costumes. Their value is not only as craft products, nor as a means of creating an illusion of reality, but as extensions of the text. They are pointers to the values of the society in which the play is set as well as additional features of the composition of the characters. Drama work in schools, though principally concerned with language and movement, should cultivate an appreciation of visual and auditory stimuli, for in communication they have a symbolic significance. When preparing a play for performance the players must be conscious of the experiences that they are structuring for their audience. They must anticipate how they will respond with all their senses and how aspects of the scene will have a special importance for them. The colour or the style of a costume will raise expectations about the wearer, the sensitively conducted buzz of background conversation can enhance the effect of an urgently whispered exchange in a crowded room as in *The Three Sisters*.

Spolin's book assists just such an appreciation; so does *Improvisation*. Many of the exercises in Brian Way's book (47), especially those concerned with developing concentration and sensitivity, can be a useful introduction to this awareness of the conscious use of sight and sound. For example, we might use the relentless beat of a metronome to heighten an action. The problem for the class would be to construct either all together or in groups or pairs such a critical situation so that the ticking heightens the effect of the playing. A scene in a restaurant invaded by Mafia agents was played in almost total silence, a fearful and unbearably violent silence among the players but all the while Radio One rattled out its inanities. The class might be asked to use sound effectively to counterpoint the action or similarly to use a visual effect. It is interesting to set out furniture, chairs, tables, maybe a screen in such a way that it appears deliberate, not haphazard. The class is asked to respond to the feel of the set. The pupils make up a scenario based upon the relationships suggested by the furniture placing – a court room, a recording studio, a bar – they will have many interpretations. The validity of their response may be tested by playing out that scenario among the furniture when the spatial relationships are realised.

The young child dresses up to satisfy his own ego, he does not aim to create a certain effect. It is easy to call to mind a husky six-year-old boy wearing a wedding dress but not moving like a woman nor in any way pretending to be one. He just liked to wear the garment. Equally the clothes selected from the dressing up box do not necessarily convey to the onlooker what role the child has adopted. Older children, however, with access to lengths of material and safety pins can create costumes. These can aim at the shape of historical costume, but it is much more fun to create a costume that says something about the person who is wearing it. In this way we lead children to a conscious appreciation of the significance of costume in drama, we extend their knowledge of the rules of the drama game within the more elaborate constraints of theatre.

Too often we concentrate upon the constructional skills of the theatre arts, how to make articles for plays, how to construct a real or model set and paint it. More important is an understanding of why these things are needed anyway, what relationship they have to the essential dramatic process, how they assist the creation of a living, significant present.

One of the prerequisites of the game of drama, as with any game, is that it proceeds with 'utmost seriousness'. This does not mean that it cannot be broken off for a laugh and then picked up again. This again is a characteristic of all games, but while they are being played the action matters. We know that if a player will not afford the game this seriousness, then he destroys the game for all, because by breaking consensus he destroys that which preserves the fabric of the invention.

One of the tasks of the teacher is to assist the ideas of the class to work in a dramatic way. In an earlier example we saw how the creation of the Fishing Club was necessary for the class because it made concrete the abstract problem they had set themselves – the task of convincing sceptics. So it happens that the creation of a setting for a play, even just by putting out chairs in a certain way, cannot merely imitate conditions of a room, an aircraft, a football terrace, but assist the very role definition. Who I am is related, we all know, to where I am. We play a different person in a reading room of a library from the person at the fairground; the definition of the constraints of the situation affect how we present ourselves. In this way ideas may be helped to work dramatically when the circumstances of the play can be made to feel right. The distinction is a fine one between this condition and over-elaboration. Often the infant school Nativity Play is a good example of how children can be overwhelmed with the trappings of theatre – wings and crowns, false beards and body makeup.

The Polish director, Grotowski, rejects the elaborate accoutrements of what he calls the 'Rich Theatre'. The reliance upon other borrowed disciplines he calls 'artistic kleptomania'[12] and sometimes a production being prepared for presentation makes his point. Pantomimes and musicals especially in some of our schools, appear to be anxious to rival the hardware of Drury Lane itself. One cannot help feeling, sometimes, that the whole affair offers diversion for some members of staff more than an education for the children involved. It is almost like attempting to simulate Wembley Stadium for a game against the local rival school. Now although a smart sports strip and good playing conditions do affect the team's approach to the game, they are no substitute for an understanding of the game and the possession of skills for playing it. Equally, the school production achieves distinction through the quality of the children's perception of what they are doing and the exercise of learned skills in a sensitive and a generous way. So it is that one returns to the importance of the players' encounters, the essential dramatic process, as the vital element in drama teaching. Any elaboration must arise from the more complex needs of communicating to a larger number, not merely from fancy or misplaced ambition.

Theatre in Education

There is some considerable debate about relationships between schools and the professional theatre, especially over the role of the Theatre in Education. The question is not just academic and does raise a number of issues that are relevant to this study of teaching drama.

These issues are clear and can be simply expressed. They are:

1 Should children go to a theatre to see a play or should the players bring the piece to the school?
2 When Theatre in Education teams visit schools what assumptions have been made about the work and the competence of those who teach the programme?
3 What is the point of theatre in communities of which the school forms a part?

The first question could well be answered from the point of view of economics which would recommend the bringing in of theatre companies to schools because it is cheaper. However, let us examine what the advantages of each experience are from the child's position, and how it affects his education.

The DES Drama Survey, already mentioned, reviews this whole field of activity in its chapter on 'Theatre for Children' and 'Children's Theatre.' Of special interest is the report of two companies upon the response of audiences of children in school and in a theatre. Many children expressed pleasure at having the play presented in the familiar surroundings of their own school hall. They enjoyed the simplicity of the presentation in staging and costume for they found the situations more 'real.' A survey of audience reactions conducted by another company found that theatre audiences 'readily accept the conventions of the theatre; they listen more intently, they laugh more readily, they react more subtly. They quickly cultivate a more sophisticated response to the nature of the theatrical experience and the ability to see the play as a whole.'[13]

The views expressed seem contradictory, but only if we insist upon maintaining that drama and theatre are separate, autonomous experiences. It can come as a refreshing surprise to see the actor's art not overshadowed by the trappings of theatre. We can appreciate the strategic play of the actors and the basic communication skills they employ. The intimacy of the performance area can reduce the sense of alienation and evident technique that is a danger of large theatres. The significance of the play, of the moment-to-moment encounters, is heightened by the newness of the occasion. It is not more real but as a model more effective.

On the other hand if we meet all these conditions in a theatre there is the chance of additional advantages. Selden in his book *Theatre Double Game* (39) introduces the concept of theatre as an institution for game-playing. The term need not apply only to the actual process, a view to which this book has subscribed all along, but also as a place: the Playhouse. It is easy to become sentimental about the theatre but the excited anticipation of an audience awaiting the start of a play is a real and infectious delight. Like the supporters of football approaching the ground with the people selling programmes and favours while the public address system can be heard from within the stadium, the playgoer shares the expectation of the thrill of the game. Each have their understanding of how the game is played, what the rules are and what their part is in the game. No matter how many games they attend, however, they will never see the same game twice for its progress is as transient as the passing time.

The occasion of the play is not important merely because it allows people to show off their clothes but because a group of people have assembled to experience a heightened example of life. The audience will need to be as sharp as the players to assist the playing of the piece. But they will be helped by the actors' language and movement and by the many other less obvious aspects of the theatre. All will be combined; lights, music, colour, shape and texture with the language and the gesture, to create the ordered expression that is the work of art.

There is no substitute for this communal celebration. It stimulates intellectually and emotionally and affirms our belief in and our security from a social reality that we spoke of in the first chapter. And this is true education and should be denied to no one, but, as with other learning, it should be introduced with care and discretion. By overfeeding we kill the taste for food, similarly by overteaching we kill the desire to learn. The richness of theatre is appreciated most when the plays are enjoyed with discernment, and this is a learned skill. We may, in the theatre, see the game of drama being played at its highest level of excellence by players of consummate skill. But to share most fully requires of us a sympathy and understanding derived from familiarity with the ways and means of the game. It is this familiarity that it is the job of the drama teacher or the actor in school to impart.

The survey from the DES that we quoted earlier talks of the relationship of theatres and schools as being in a 'honeymoon period' that 'is nearly over'. The goodwill from each side has become strained by their mutual lack of understanding of the purpose and value of theatre in education. Far too often actors feel threatened by the lack of credibility their work encounters among teachers. They are not seriously considered as contributing to children's education but are regarded as hired entertainers. For the school's part they take exception, and rightly, to actors being sent into schools 'with the idea that it is for them to brighten education'.[14] Teachers sometimes envy the human and material resources of the programmes and the time available for their preparation. They wonder that with such a headstart the achievement in the classroom can be so slight and superficial. They watch actors whose warmth and sensitivity has captured the attention and commitment of a class, destroy the fabric of what has been created by poor questioning or dogmatic, authoritarian views. They do not know the tyranny of the length of the session and the compulsion to win approval with successful results. Nor do they know of the weary and demanding tours of schools that require loading in the early morning and rehearsing late in the evening of the same day having played the programme sometimes in three different schools.

It is more than knowing the working conditions of each other that will ensure mutual respect. Above all it must be more clearly understood in what way actors can be of value to the education of the child. It certainly is not by presenting quick and ready topic examinations of pollution, delinquency, mental health, the Romans or the Third World in attractive dramatic packages. What actors can do so superbly is to show through their skills how drama is 'a means of making a profound personal comment on facts, events, ideas, relationships that are the very stuff of human existence. They can demonstrate a highly developed form of play in the children's own terms'.[15] They can reveal how the dramatic process works so that children may be encouraged to use it as a natural expressive form. They may help teachers not by telling them how to teach, but by extending their understanding of how they can help their pupils' ideas to be realised dramatically.

It has not been in drawing attention to already well publicised national and international themes that the Theatre in Education teams have enjoyed their greatest successes, but in their presentation of issues of local interest. Archive material has provided documentary plays that have given insights into the rise and fall of local industries, the fortunes of the local football club over the years, the changing social conditions of people in the area and the problems of transport, housing, etc. The programme in Coventry that considered the occupation of the area by the Romans culminated in a visit to the partially restored fort at Bagington, nearby. Seldom can schoolchildren have been better prepared for a field visit, for previously they had, unwittingly, chosen that very spot for building their fort from a study of a relief model. Their reasons for building at that place were just the same as those of their Roman predecessors. The actors had used this device to create the setting in which children could feel committed to the game of exploring the relationships between the occupier and the occupied.

The actor/teacher teams, a term of dubious validity, have undertaken what is part of the responsibility of theatre but which is neglected so often. This duty is to give expression to the life of the community, to present the events of that life as significant. In this way the teams have rediscovered the purpose of theatre and already feel restricted in having to confine the work to schools. Many of the teams feel the need to spread their work more widely through the community of which the school is a part. In fact they wish to serve the true function of the theatre in society.

The latter part of this chapter has not been a diversion from the consideration of the teaching of drama to children. It has been an attempt to present a picture of the links that do exist and should exist with the world outside the school. The incidence of Theatre in Education provides a half-way house in such a study. The Epilogue will, briefly, relate the teaching to an even wider purpose for the teaching of the art of drama.

The heritage of dramatic literature and the continuance of the theatre as a means of serving social needs – these are rich studies that no drama teacher should deny his pupils. Doctrinaire theories that rob the drama of any connection with these riches impoverish children and stunt the development that is so anxiously but sometimes mistakenly pursued by drama teachers. But we must preserve the learning as an active process through constant and enjoyable practice of the game of drama.

Summary

The discipline of the drama is related to the study of the text and to the experience of the play in performance. It stresses the importance of the closest links between drama teaching and the study of dramatic literature and theatre. Finally it reviews the relationship of the professional theatre to the work of the school and how they may be mutually benefited by greater understanding of each other's separate strengths.

Notes

1 Duncan (52)
2 Williams (50) page 38
3 Fergusson (8) page 238
4 Stanislavski (45) page 112
5 Brook (5) page 120
6 Stanislavski (45) page 254
7 Pinter (38) page 24
8 Brook (5) page 124
9 Brook (5) page 100
10 Hodgson(16) page 164
11 Spolin (44) page 13
12 Grotowski (14) page 14
13 DES (54) page 99
14 DES (54) page 97
15 DES (54) page 98

Further Reading

Spolin (44)
Stanislavski (45)
Brook (5)
Hodgson and Richards (17)
Grotowski (14)
Selden (39)
Bentley (3)
Fergusson (8)

The books listed above represent writings of thinkers in the theatre. Stanislavski (45), Grotowski (14) and Brook (5), three great directors, give insights into their work with actors assisting the creative process. Spolin (44) and Hodgson and Richards (17) extend the approach into work that is applicable directly to the school situation. Bentley (3) and Fergusson (8), scholars and men of the theatre offer brilliant insights into the art of drama while Selden (39) introduces the concept of the theatre as an institution for games playing, a central feature of the argument of this book.

9

Drama and the School Play

The School Play

Although the School Play must be the most familiar of dramatic activities in schools, it would not be easy to find much support for it among Drama in Education teachers. Undoubtedly it gives satisfaction to participating staff and pupils and to parents and friends, especially when the production is ended and all the hard work is behind everyone; when their labours seem crowned with success and their intentions realised. Furthermore it commands, as an activity, often more prestige, appreciation and support than the day to day pursuit of Drama as a method of class teaching and learning. It would seem sensible, therefore, to make a reappraisal of the School Play and to examine in what ways it complements or conflicts with those views of Drama that we have presented earlier.

The indictment against the School Play is a fairly formidable one especially if one questions its educational purpose. Rarely do we expect school children to perform such feats in the field of sports as are expected in their theatre. The attempting of Greek tragedy or the great plays of Shakespeare is not uncommon in our secondary schools, while *Oliver, My Fair Lady, Oh What a Lovely War*, etc are becoming standard fare among school presentations. This may be because it is assumed that the level of skills required to play top class rugby football or cricket is not required for an attempt at theatre. Even if a school did have some classes in acting skills, the standard required for such portrayals as Agamemnon, Hamlet or Eliza Doolittle requires years of training. It seems most likely, then, that the successful production emerges more from skilful direction than from accomplished acting. In other words the children animate the teacher's vision of the play in all its parts through intense drill and good memory. Nor is this to deny that there is merit in the exercise or that the participants do not gain some insights into the art of drama that they might not get otherwise. What is certain however is that productions of the sort mentioned above are teacher-centred, teacher directed and teacher dominated. Children are not consulted about the decisions that surround the presentation nor about what sorts of experiences they aim to build either for the audience or themselves.

Nor are these enterprises confined to the secondary school, for the Nativity Play and the Summer Concert with music and drama on the programme is common enough in the primary School. Here, again, the plays represent the expression of sympathetic teachers with some experience and perhaps training in theatre. Sometimes it is merely someone whose turn it is this year or an edict that each class will perform.

One would like to believe that musicians have at least sufficient respect for their art that they expect some musical knowledge as a prerequisite, though even here presumably conditioning can work wonders. Rarely, however, does the acting match the singing or even the instrumental performance in the music part of a concert or musical. Drama teachers have no such qualms but make do with astute casting so that the production exploits the natural characteristics of the children in the cast, a familiar feature of amateur dramatics. The sensitive, imaginative teacher can work wonders with such a technique and with the support of a well dressed show can produce work that is a credit to the school. Certainly the parents who attend the play have the assurance that their children attend a school with standards of accomplishment, a school which sets a tone that can benefit the ambitious child or parent.

Nor are any of these remarks intended to be derisive nor seek to denigrate either such parents or such a school. It is reassuring to see all sections of the school united in such a venture though to assume that it represents its usual cohesion or purpose is perhaps rather optimistic. Nevertheless the School Play does take its place alongside public examinations, successful sports records, uniform, prize-giving and a well academically qualified Head and Staff as a desirable feature of an educationally sound establishment.

It is from this doubtful position that many drama teachers have found a toehold in the rock face of the curriculum and established the subject in a more worthwhile form. However, once the school has a name for good theatre, in the traditional sense, it is often hard to change the sort of programme that has gained the classroom drama its admittance. Indeed where teachers have attempted to present their pupils' own plays, the subject matter, often controversial, receives an amused tolerance but seldom enthusiasm. This is sad for as we shall see later such an expressive form for adolescents in particular could speak to adults and particularly parents in an incomparable way. It is likely also that in such a presentation the cast will be composed of at least some members of the school who do not represent its most successful pupils either academically or in the sporting sphere. Too often the traditional school play features in its main parts children who are successful in other spheres and who are the school's cream. Their ability to speak clearly and present an acceptable appearance contributes to that overall view of the school as firmly part of the establishment that we referred to earlier.

The School Play, then, is essentially an extra-curricular presentation, the product of voluntary participation, generally in the mainstream of our cultural traditions. It is representative of the overall tone of the establishment but does not have any structured educational objectives, nor does it impinge upon the general life of the school except in so far as its demand for space and rehearsal time get greater as the date of the presentation approaches. It rarely is related to the curriculum nor to any expression of the life of the school. It emerges from the teacher's choice, invariably, and conforms with his vision with no attempt at involving the children in any dialogue concerning its appropriateness to their lives or experience.

It would be cynical in the extreme to suggest that the School Play is regarded as simply a bit of window dressing and has no benefits directly for the children taking part. As mentioned earlier there is a deal of satisfaction gained from a well executed piece, though, again, it must be said that it is doubtful whether these derivatives are to be obtained only from this source. What claims might one make to justify the considerable effort and expense that the School Play demands?

First there is the set, achievable goal which demands a genuine group responsibility, loyalty and perseverance. Then there is the opportunity for work that involves the feelings, the affective area of the child's being. Then there is the confidence imbued by that trial by ordeal that is the public performance. Teachers appreciate the opportunity of a more relaxed relationship with pupils, feeling that each appreciates the other more as a person and a colleague in the joint practical venture. The self-discipline that performance requires is yet another feature that recommends the exercise, for both off and on stage the need to place one's own needs below those of the group is paramount, and often difficult to achieve.

No-one would deny that these things do happen and are often offered as the educational justification for a very time and energy consuming operation. What is certainly not true would be that these benefits are the exclusive property of the drama. Many of them could justifiably be claimed by other group pastimes in sport or other leisure activities. It could be claimed that they are achieved and with far less fuss and disruption. After all very often the School Play demands the help of the home economics department, the music department, the craft department, the art department and the physics teacher. Sometimes where sympathy and enthusiasm exists the co-operation is welcomed but sometimes it represents a frustrating postponement of the normal education programme in order to accommodate these additional demands. Nor do these aspects of production exhaust the list; ticket sellers, refreshment makers, front of house, car park organisation, the list goes on.

To subsume the outcomes under the name of Education is a doubtful claim for it must be very seldom that the whole operation is conceived of as a learning experience, especially as the children have so little part in it as planners or indeed assessors. The only way in which the term could be used would be only very widely to imply something that was for the general well being of the child. Such vagueness is not likely to afford the School Play as Drama a great deal of respect or indeed recognition among the other curriculum subjects. There still exists in the secondary school the view that however good chaps they may be, the drama and physical education teachers run a pretty soft option with art, music, craft and home economics not far behind.

To begin to detail the shortcomings of the infant school Nativity Play or to describe the processes of the junior school concert would not advance the argument any further and only seem to pursue malicious ends. Suffice it to say that the anguish that accompanies the production in the secondary school is much worse in the primary school if only because the smaller staff complement are invariably involved inescapably as are often every child in every class, willing or not.

Rather than persist with this negative view it would be better to explore what alternatives exist that confer the same benefits but with an additional *bone fide* educational content. In order to do this we will draw on many points that we have made earlier and especially the view that the experience of the creative and performing arts for children must involve a genuine creative input from them and that the play should exist as a vehicle for the expression of the child's concerns.

Play making
If public performance is the intention then it would seem obvious that either as a class or as a theatre workshop group children should be invited to consider what they would wish to show. Even more fundamental questions can be asked such as whether to perform a scripted play or whether to improvise, should the play involve all as actors or only a few, will the play be essentially a simple presentation or do the children see the exercise as an

elaborate one, for that will bring a whole new train of considerations. Further questions might involve what is the experience one is hoping the audience will have, what sorts of things do you wish them to think about? None of these seem redundant questions but it must be very seldom that they are asked of a potential cast.

A class of ten to eleven year olds were invited to make a play of their own to perform in public. Confident in the ways and means of the drama game, they were well aware of what the task would involve when they chose to make a simple play that involved everyone as actors but which would rely almost entirely upon their own skills to evoke location and properties. Very simple timeless and placeless costumes were to complete the visual expression of the piece.

The class were reminded that drama is not the animation of a story but the representation of people who face a dilemma not merely circumstantial but which in a particular circumstance will involve them making a decision based upon moral values. This definition was conveyed in simple language and seems to offer no difficulty. The class was then invited to form self-chosen groups to seek for an example of such a dilemma. From the four groups emerged a play about a group of travellers some of whose members have fallen into a deep pit. Rescue attempts were unsuccessful and time wasting and the dilemma that faced the group was whether to leave them and so preserve their own lives or whether to stay and persist with their attempts at saving their fellows. Another group described a people struck with a fatal illness, the healthy were faced with the dilemma of whether to abandon the sick and dying to save themselves. Much the same problem faced another group except in this case there was a known cure. This resided in an incredible plant the fetching of which involved almost certain death so fearful was the journey. The dilemma then was whether the fit and well should risk their lives for the sick and dying. The last suggestion involved a set of twin brothers mistaken for their criminal other halves having to prove innocence – a situational dilemma not a moral and also a play intended for the small group and not the whole class as previously determined.

The teacher discussed with the class the implications of the suggestions and why they thought it would make a good play. The play involving the incredible plant was thought by the class to be the most promising, because as one girl said, it was a play worth doing because it involved people being prepared to sacrifice themselves for others. It was later to be called, *The Choice* for as the play developed it became clearer that this was the hub of the play, the preparedness of the villagers to lay down their lives for their friends and their enemies.

It was decided that the opening of the play should establish the village and its life and particularly the tensions that existed between rival families. This was accomplished by showing the villagers going to work in the early morning, a quiet opening with an intense feel by the class for the pace and volume of the piece. Gradually each increased from an almost silent passage of knots of people preparing for the day's labours. This was achieved by the teacher's invitation to discuss the quality of the early morning and how to represent it. Children were not drilled in something they had not themselves suggested or created. The desired effect was never difficult to reproduce in rehearsal for the cast was aware what it wanted the audience to feel and how to obtain it.

As the village came alive and got to work a dispute arose between two groups of men about a suspected theft of wood. The bitter argument attracted onlookers and eventually resulted in a brief fight interrupted by the village elder who condemned the behaviour as anti-social and with the backing of the village demanded a return to work. This explosive opening was not unlike the settling of the civil brawl in *Romeo and Juliet* but without its penalties. The villagers resumed their labours but only to be interrupted by the sudden illness of various members who quickly died, a moment of theatre as the concern for the sickness became the sorrow and the shock of death. The bodies were buried and the village then assembled for the formal debate of their position. Among the circle the elder presided with the staff in his hand that conferred the right to speak. People came forward to take the staff and offer their opinions on the cause of the mysterious deaths and what might cure the sickness. Eventually it was recalled that once before when the village had been so threatened the incredible plant had proved the saviour but only a few returned with the plant from the search.

It was agreed that the plant should be fetched and people nominated to go but these nominations were rejected by the parties named because they refused to give their lives for this family or that who had wronged them down the years. When there seemed deadlock an impassioned condemnation of this selfishness was made by a villager who offered himself as the first volunteer. Others followed including those shamefaced who had previously declined. The party set off amid applause and urgent requests to take care and come back safely. The choice had been made between individual preservation of life, face and family pride and a selfless preparedness to risk all for one's fellows. The simple theme was affecting and especially played with such total conviction as these children felt and communicated.

At every step the relationships had been lived through in improvisation and then the question posed how was this to be shown in such a way as to be understood. The proof could be tested only one way and that as in the realisation of the intention; the thought in action. Again as we said earlier the question was not 'Is this good?' so much as 'Does this work?' Also although the piece was repeated in the classroom to prepare it for public presentation, it was never exactly the same twice running but in following the determined pattern admitted genuine improvisation, like a good jazz band.

When the time came to costume the piece a number of odds and ends of lengths of materials, tunics, etc, were put out on tables and the children invited to sort out their own apparel. The result was staggeringly effective and was regularly reproduced whenever required.

The public performance was competent despite insufficient time for trying out the new acting space. Most admirably the class maintained its remarkable poise, adapting to the varying spaces available, again and again. Despite the pressure of the occasion the cast still was able to maintain a freshness and even an originality. The audiences expecting less thought provoking or original work, and also needing to hear more carefully, were appreciative, but not provoked, as maybe was part of the intention. Most important, however, was that the goal had been achieved and with a preparation that provoked among these children of different ethnic backgrounds a moral discussion that would not have shamed the Socratic dialogues of Plato.

All the beneficial qualities ascribed to the School Play were present here, together with less fuss and much more active and controlled learning. The class with the teacher's assistance had made the decisions and realised them through the drama game. This could be partly ascribed to the fact that the play was part of the total education in the class for these children, and indeed gained immeasurably for the normal conduct of affairs in the classroom where discussion of the children's suggestions occurred continually. People were taught to listen to each other and respect other's views. This generosity revealed itself in the play through the apparent skill of performance. The insecurity of improvisation was offset by strength of the inter-personal trust and total absence of either competition or personal desire to be noticed. That rapport that exists in good adult actors, particularly in the best professional presentations, was present with the juvenile cast not because they were skilled actors but because they were generous, feeling people with respect and affection for each other and pride in the work in hand.

Many people would not disagree that such cohesion is possible within the primary school, where teachers and pupils share so much of their time that a greater family feeling is achieved. The secondary school class and the secondary school child is a different kettle of fish. The secondary class does not spend all its time together but splits up for sets or different subjects, are often already in classes that reflect their academic ability, and are rarely with one teacher for very long. The circumstances are not very favourable for work that calls for a socially healthy group. However, many teachers have shown, through their concern and respect for the children, that using timetabled time or with supplemented free time voluntarily contributed by the class, that such work is possible. Inded they would claim that the work involved nurtured the social health of the group. Like the experience of an Outdoor Pursuit Centre, a camp, or foreign trip, the growth of real personal relationships, including with the teacher, is very evident.

Youth Theatre

More often than not, however, the play emerges from a Theatre Workshop, an extra-timetabled activity that enables children committed to the work to explore with a teacher in a relaxed atmosphere, a variety of drama approaches including the play for public presentation. As described earlier the same basic approach to discovering the concerns of the group is possible, and the realisation of them through drama into theatre performance. Nor are such groups confined to schools but appear as Children's Theatre Groups or Youth Theatre, a number of which flourish in London and up and down the country. The reputation they have gained for themselves has encouraged established playwrights to work with them to add to the presentations they give from the wider dramatic literature repertoire.

The work of the Birmingham Youth Theatre under Derek Nicholls and Ray Speakman, particularly well-known to me, must rank with the best anywhere. This is not said in any parochial sense of competition but simply to give due regard to its achievement and especially as its methods follow closely those we have outlined in most cases. This company is recruited from volunteers nominated by teachers from Birmingham schools and performs in the studio of the Birmingham Repertory Theatre and sometimes tours the productions to local schools and colleges. Its two directors held senior posts as English teachers and are accomplished writers whose work had been performed both by professional theatre companies and on television, often as especially commissioned pieces.

First and foremost, however, the directors are accomplished teachers whose understanding of working with children ensures that there are genuine, educational benefits enjoyed. The casts change so that a good number of children are introduced to the Youth Theatre's work, the presentational standard of which is of the highest order. Particularly interesting, however, is the range of topics explored, which includes young people working in a bakery, *Baker's Boy: In Your Own Time,* a play about truancy; *Run Rabbit,* evacuees in Wales during World War Two; *The House Gang,* a play about a group of adolescents who use a derelict house as their headquarters; *Sleepers* a play built from extended contact with homeless young people in the city's night shelters, and more; the list is in no way exhaustive.

The plays were remarkable for the clarity of the expression of a young person's point of view. As an adult member of the audience, one might sense that one recalled the feeling expressed from one's own youth. At other times one was surprised by a perspective that was entirely unfamiliar and refreshingly new. The sympathy that such work evoked in adults for the concerns of young people was intense. Nevertheless it was sufficiently forthright and outspoken to evoke the usual criticism of theme and language. There never was any irresponsibility from the cast or directors in this area, but always a careful decision was made about the acceptability of material. The basis for the decision was one of artistic integrity and not merely sensational.

The method working is by now established; the cast assemble and become familiar with each other through drama games and more extended improvisions. Themes are discussed and explored and gradually a shape emerges assisted by the perception and the awareness of theatrical potential by the two directors. They make notes through the sessions and incorporate the themes and their expression into script form. This provides a blueprint for the play and is mutable up to a certain point in time. Thereafter the play is rehearsed and polished in that form that seems most satisfactory to all. This combination of young ideas with adult feeling for the discipline of the form results in presentations of great power. Rarely have adults taken part as players so that adults' roles are portrayed by these adolescent schoolchildren. Universally their portrayals reveal an immense compassion that seems to make nonsense of the claims of the inevitability of a generation gap. It is sad, indeed, that adult playwrights and actors do not generally seem to have that same compassionate insight into the feelings of young people, but perhaps that will emerge one day.

The Birmingham Youth Theatre continues its excellent work at the Midlands Arts Centre, a most appropriate venue with its accent upon providing for young people. New casts will assemble and the work will reflect their concerns, but the high standards remain for the directors have a clear understanding of what they are doing and why. Their sympathy and trust in their young actors and technicians will be amply rewarded by the intense commitment of the Company to the work.

This central role of the directors of the Birmingham Youth Theatre has to be acknowledged as it often must in similar companies. Invariably such people count amoung their experience a successful period of classroom teaching, not always as exclusively drama teachers. It might seem then that we might add to this review how, within the teacher training programme, we might include such work, not as the support of a superannuated dramatic society, but a genuine educational experience for the student as person and teacher; the two being inseparable.

Teacher training

As was mentioned at the very beginning of the book, the decline in numbers of teachers needed and the economic restrictions exercised, has resulted in many undergraduate BEd courses almost entirely eliminating the contribution of the arts in any major sense. Increasingly the DES concentrates only on the shortage subjects of maths, science, crafts and music but always within the traditional pattern of the curriculum as the transference of information rather than the subject as learning facilitator. The result of this emphasis is to restrict other areas of study and especially those areas that seem less central to core curriculum studies themselves invariably dictated by public examinations.

Prospects for the sort of training being suggested may seem bleak in the short term but it does not invalidate the argument. In those years of expansion in a number of teacher training establishments as John Allen records in his book, *Drama in Schools* valuable work was done and, as with the Youth Theatre, will remain as a powerful medium for instruction when wiser counsels prevail.

The DES in its report 'Aspects of the curriculum in Secondary Schools' criticises the teaching methods, perhaps rightly commenting that what results in schools as teacher/pupil exchange reflects the shortcomings of the training establishment. Also perhaps the lack of self-appraisal, the inability to see the curriculum as a whole emerges from the same source. This would result from that same fragmentation that we find in schools where teachers are unaware of student experience except in their own area.

This approach encourages the student to regard each activity on the timetable as self-contained and separate while the uniting influence of Educational Studies has been notoriously absent. There has been an immense failure, by and large, not only to relate theory to practice but also theory to theory as enshrined in the contributing disciplines. In this respect the scrutiny of the CNAA has proved valuable in assisting institutions to present their submissions for the professional preparation as coherent programmes.

It would be ridiculous to suggest that drama teaching should be excluded from the indictment of teacher training in the sixties and seventies. Too often the work was essentially the same as that of many a student amateur dramatic society but with staff direction and expertise and greater injections of financial assistance resulting in impressive theatres, scenery, costumes, lighting systems, etc. The professional preparation of the teacher existed as a separate input and often condemned connection between the two. The former was claimed as being formative in the student's personal education, with some justification, the latter a part of his professional preparation but the two were not combined. Though one might imagine that such a division would by now be thought to be ridiculous, the constraints attending the degree programmes that stress the degree worthiness of the studies have ensured the maintenance of this unfortunate situation. From the drama point of view it encouraged those different categories we mentioned earlier and denied appreciation of the public performance as an essential and valid educational pursuit closely allied with the classroom experience.

In his book *Hopes of Great Happenings*, Albert Hunt described the work in Bradford which was to become so famous and which was discontinued for much the same reasons we have already discussed. Although these were not teachers in training their experience can be related directly to the classroom preparation under review. The methods of information gathering, selecting and living through in dramatic exploration is appropriate for many ages of people and many purposes.

My own experience of playmaking with student teachers has convinced me of the numerous benefits that result from the work. Equally our presentations of established dramatic work, was always intended to enhance not only the appropriate skills for theatre practice but also the pedagogic. A production of the *Cuchulain Saga* of Yeats emerged from those same questions put to students as were put to the cast of *The Choice*. Their preference was for a scripted play – they had done mostly improvised work previously – one which would include them all as actors, technicians

129

etc. and for a play which would allow the audience to observe its totality, not a theatre of illusion. Their hunt through plays to find an appropriate one, introduced them to a great variety of authors. When someone found, *The Homecoming* and was on fire to do it, the class had to decide whether it lay within their criteria and if not whether they should be changed. They rejected such a move and Pinter was postponed. Once the saga was agreed upon as an appropriate choice, where it should be played and how were pressing questions. The studio with its remote control board for lighting, its sound equipment, etc, was rejected, for the students felt they would be unlikely to find such conditions in schools, and wanted this to be a preparation for their possible involvement with school plays, once they were qualified. So they chose the College hall which, except for its beautiful wood floor, was not so well endowed for the presentation of plays as many a school hall. In order to preserve their intentions, the students decided to sit the audience on the raised stage, banking the seating down to the hall floor level. The play used a simple platform with two poles like lamp standards which held the lights, operated through simple slide dimmers and using electricity from the ring main system. The loading had to be carefully worked out and a plot constructed. A mistake once involved repairing the fuse during a short interval, not a difficult task but one demanding cool heads at that time and a thorough knowledge of how the system worked.

The audience and the cast sat in a horseshoe around the hall floor, the back of the horseshoe being raised some three feet or so to the stage level. The very extremes of the horseshoe were occupied on the one side by the cast and on the other the musicians and the simple lighting position, all in full view but having to take care not to distract. This again imposed the need for intense self discipline and the relegation of personal recognition to the group identity and the group task.

The students and I had discussed music and I favoured Ravi Shanka. They rejected the suggestion being more aware than I that at that time the sitar was being exploited by pop musicians and would have given the wrong stimulus. Instead they asked whether they might have a derelict piano and write their own score. The piano was dismembered and the strings on their frame extracted. There followed a series of exciting experiments to find noises that twanged, buzzed, growled and so on, to accompany the mystery of *At the Hawks Well*, or the violence of, *The Death of Cuchulain*. With the help of a student taking music as a main course and drama as subsidiary, the cast learned how to write a score that was like one of Stockhausen. The visual representation enabled anyone thereafter to reproduce the music which came largely from the piano wires but also had small drums and a recorder. The effect was electrifying and simple enough to be encouraged in schools where the music in education movement with John Paynter's *Sound and Silence* can lend support.

The costumes were equally exciting emerging from a decision to maintain simplicity. A basic strip was worn by all, tee shirt top and trousers in dark colours. The rest of the dress was derived from bolts of material that could be worn as skirts, shawls, cloaks, togas, etc. These were secured by chunky home-made jewellery inspired by a visit to the costumes of the television series Henry VIII. Bottle tops and corrugated paper among other materials became the pins that secured the garments together with almost all the spare wide webbing belts from the local fire station. Prayers were offered nightly that no large conflagration would find firemen bereft of trouser support!

An actor would leave the platform and as he descended leave his role. He would unpin his cloak and be met by another character having left her seat amid the audience. He would exchange the material which would become a skirt by the adoption of a belt. Not only were the techniques on display but the overall tone of the materials and colours maintained a unity.

Here, then was the presentation of a scripted play serving a defined educational purpose. Because the project had grown out of a carefully built consensual base, its performance was powerful and full of confidence. The speaking of the script was worked upon with equal care not only for the quality of the language but also for the thought expressed. The rehearsal had been intense but using four separate casts for the major roles in the four plays made the rehearsal schedules easier without needless attendance.

I have dwelt at length upon the scripted play because it offers great difficulties. As interesting were the plays that arose from the group as expressions of their own concern. The subjects varied widely; *Somewhere over the Rainbow* a play about the phoney war set in a cinema in 1939; *Everything is Beautiful* a play made and shown in one week as a Field Work exercise. It dealt with rising redundancy and was an angry rejection of unemployment that was affecting the students' familes. *And Was Jerusalem* was a play that took a documentary form and called attention to the condition of workers in heavy industry today, through a look at the past hundred years of industrial working conditions. It resulted from visits we had made to a coal mine, blast furnaces, the Potteries, etc. The use of archive material and oral history from family and friends was particularly effective. In Canada a group of students made a play that dealt with the local townsfolk's attitude to the hitch hikers on the Trans-Canada highway nearby and another group in Toronto played *Talking of Changes* a play that

131

examined the decline of traditional norms and values and the breaking up of second and third generation Canadian immigrant families. Some students in this country who thoughtlessly espoused the cause of a teacher's strike were given a day long exercise to make a play about the dispute but presenting all points of view. The morning was spent sifting information in groups – parents, teachers, LEAs. Then followed a simulated public meeting where the various parties presented these views in debate. Finally a sort of 'Nationwide' programme, with great licence, was presented in the evening. The cleverly selected items all were representative of the slogan of the time, 'Teachers need more Pay' though now supported by fact and considered opinion.

One of the most memorable plays that were made was, *Oh You Lucky People*, for it emerged from a group that was divided initially and in bad social health. For ages their endeavours to bring together some agreed theme foundered. Well worked pieces went no further, each session began badly, moved into a productive phase and then ended with no real progress having been made. The problem lay in finding a form that would accommodate their various needs; some for a rather showy theatrical experience, others for a more socially committed play, serious and simple.

One day before class began a group were reading horoscopes and it was from here that agreement came. The play would show the turns of the Wheel of Fortune whose predictions shown under the various signs and houses told the fortunes of people under Health, Wealth, Love and Marriage, etc. A number of situations were explored in improvisation, the common factor being that all the people were losers. The play contrasted the superficiality of the horoscope forecasts with the reality of the lives of unfortunate people. This compassion for the disadvantaged had existed all along but the work was too fragmented to come together in a coherent form.

The setting was a fairground and the Wheel of Fortune a major feature. The audience entered the Studio through an experience tunnel, a House of Horrors; spiders' webs and tableaux luridly lit presenting werewolves, etc. All the time could be heard the music of the fairground and as one reached the tunnel's end it was to be enveloped in noise, lights and music. A number of booths were scattered about and a crowd, the cast, perambulated. The main stand was the great Wheel of Fortune glittering and gawdy. Before it was being conducted a talent contest with all the patter but no apparent play in the usual sense. The talent contest winner was rewarded with a free fortune forecast and the great wheel spun and the flashy mini-skirted assistants performed under the direction of the Barker. The forecast delivered, the assistants passed among the crowd gathered about, the audience by now were seated on a bank of seats at the rear and sides. Envelopes were sold for cash rather like those of a racing tipster, some lucky people would win a Spin of the Wheel. These people identified, the wheel spun for the first time – the House of Health. The lights descended, a curtain drew to obscure the booth and the first set of scenes began. Four or five spins followed interspersed by the Barker's patter. When all was done a new talent contest was being drummed up and the whole thing began all over again, while the audience left through the tunnel.

There was a curious sense of being cheated by the play, of being a loser but also the satisfaction of seeing this as part of its intention, to create a bond with the material. The scenes had a cumulative significance though none related directly to another. Some scenes, especially one that showed the loneliness and confusion of a young person amid the drug culture of the time was painful to watch but very revealing to an older generation. The overall fairground symbol was good because it reflected how much we want to be convinced of luck and good fortune and how often it is an illusion. The play was a sad one overall though there were very funny scenes. The young people who made it were not optimistic and found the world in which they felt they had to compete a rather tasteless one.

The presentation was elaborate but in a way that involved an audience, very carefully set and dressed but having an impression of being rather tatty and gimcrack. The language at times reached a rare degree of poetic spirit not often present in improvised work which can be prosaic in the extreme. Above all its totality was understood by each member of the cast because he had constructed the piece both in practical and theoretical terms. It was no mere coincidence that a number of students of that year subsequently achieved distinguished work in theatre with children in the schools where they taught.

Perhaps we might end with this concentration upon the contribution of the individual to the group purpose and the sense of understanding of the project felt by everyone connected with it. Too often the purpose of the play is not merely misunderstood by a cast but something of which they are entirely ignorant. Equally what happens to prepare and run the play technically is a mystery. In the sorts of work used as illustration it must be abundantly clear that the working methods rely upon a group understanding and each person's commitment to it. The results of such working for public presentation can be very forceful and entertaining. The skills of the dramatist too become much clearer as with practical experience of theatre, one can the better recognise the part of the playwright's art that reveals his work as being theatrically possible as well as potent literature.

The School Play which is often the cause of many misgivings can be an agent of great educational worth when imbued with those qualities and characteristics we have ascribed to the Drama Game throughout the book.

Summary
This chapter argues the educational advantages of the School Play. Especially it commends the task as a focus for an exploration of social values and attitudes. These may be contained within a script or are discernible in an improvised scene. Their communication to an audience involves a sensitive use of theatre arts where the form and the meaning are creatively allied.

10

Drama and Community Arts

An interesting development among the Arts and one closely allied to Education, is the area known as Community Arts. Among Community Artists themselves there is great debate about its exact nature and purposes, the criteria for assessment and its relationship to the traditional art forms. In this book, therefore, we shall not pursue those questions in any depth respecting the primacy of the practitioners to speak to their work. However, and hoping not to be thought presumptious, we can make some observations and particularly insofar as the work resembles what we have already talked about and where its educational purposes take it beyond its own pursuits.

A major reason for such a review is that drama plays an important part in the Community Arts programmes where with adults, mainly, it performs some of the functions we have described, but also some interesting additional ones. One suspects that with the increase of unemployment among young and old the sorts of concerns promoted by this group of dedicated artists may well come to prove a very much more familiar feature of our society.

The movement if not overtly politically sympathetic certainly is deeply socially committed. The artists seek to serve those who are powerless through ignorance of how they are being exploited, ignored, or are victims of a negative discrimination. The areas in which such people live tend to be the inner city houses with poor amenities and badly neglected, or upon the faceless estates to which people have been moved in urban rehousing programmes. They often suffer communally the disadvantages resulting from bad planning of bad national or local government. But rarely do they enjoy a communal spirit or have the cohesive strength to sue for changes in their conditions: a children's playground, a new bus stop, a hospital. Such apparent apathy is often ascribed to their lack of intelligence or meagre education. Yet the former is rarely the answer and if their education has been meagre it is a result of a bad system that disenchants its pupils. More likely is the lack of self confidence and self awareness that accompanies being a persistent loser, or at least being constantly told that you are a failure. Some artists will give a political analysis of such a situation and see their work as being part of the struggle of the proleteriat. Others may see simply the need to bring what skills they have to the aid of underprivileged people.

The arts, it is felt, are a valuable part of life that if not actually denied the people in question, nevertheless are often inaccessible partly because of the mystique that so often surrounds their practice. It is the intention of Community Arts that all should enjoy the arts as creative participants and appreciate the work of artists and craftsmen, actors and musicians. The aesthetic plays a vital part also in the everyday environment of the home and neighbourhood and the encouragement of people to enhance the visual aspects of their surroundings again will be part of the movement. Community Radio attempts to be more discerning about the programmes relayed on cable radio on estates and gives people the opportunity to make their own programmes; more of that later. Crafts enable this aesthetic quality to be a part of the home, and community writing persuades people to try the written expression of their experience.

There is, then, the intention to encourage an appreciation and participation in the arts in the traditional sense. There is also the socio political aim which is to build the sense of community; the sharing of experience, the ability to negotiate meaning, to act in concert to achieve communal ends and to consider the good of the group rather than the selfish satisfaction of the individual where such satisfaction is to be had only at the expense of others. The arts in this context are the expressive voice of the community, the artist 'the spike in the side of the community' stimulating it to challenge itself. Through creative work, group created, can come the sense of community and/or from a sense of community can come the strong artistic statement of its needs, its beliefs, its achievements.

I have been privileged to be involved in the encouragement of Community Arts in the West Midlands through the Regional Arts Association. The responsibility of funding the various projects has taken me to see work of immensely high standards of execution and dedication and of great variety. Again where the work of the various groups is mentioned, it is not to claim a regional superiority but simply to illustrate the principles.

Projects

The scene is an old primary school amid the space which was once terraced houses in an inner part of Birmingham. There is a nursery class at play with a multiracial mix of whites, blacks and Asian children. In another room the mothers sit at a long table making Christmas decorations with the assistance of a community artist, herself a very accomplished potter. The class appears to resemble the same sort of busy group you might find in the Women's Institute or adult evening class. However there is a difference for although the women gain great pleasure from the items as they come to completion, the artist's work does not end there. With skilful questions she encourages not only their conversation but also encourages them towards the planning of a Christmas Fayre. She does not impose her own ideas at any time but helps the group to persist in its purpose, maintaining the focus of the conversation and drawing together its conclusions. There is a deal of controversy about prices, rotas, particular functions, but it all concludes successfully with the group feeling satisfied and fulfilled. All the while the artist has been quietly assisting the craft work, declining to be judge or arbiter in the conversation but always demonstrating her unquestioned faith in the group to succeed. The role sounds not at all unlike those functions of the teacher in the classroom that we have described where healthy social relationships are nurtured and genuine learning takes place. One of the mothers, a vital and talkative young woman described to me how before bringing her child to the nursery and joining the craft group she had been fearful of leaving the house and would not go shopping unless accompanied, a not uncommon condition among such mothers.

Another development recounted to me was of two men one in middle age, a car worker, and another younger man later to be joined by a young woman, who came to the community artists to enquire about the price of 'Rent-a-clown' for a children's party. The cost was beyond their means so they implored the artists, expert in film, photography and screen printing, but also performers, to fill their bill. The artists refused but said they would assist the men to work up their own show if they wished. So was born a group that not only played to audiences of many ages but who also met regularly to rehearse new material and to discuss a whole array of topics. The artists did not instruct but assisted the invention. They did not impose their views but carefully brought the group to examine what lay behind their comedy which was often both sexist and racist. The artists did not condemn but simply assisted such perceptions to be discovered. The clowning then involved a high degree of skill which sometimes was taught but the content was also important because it was social comment. The responsibility of the performer was being encouraged as well as his expertise.

In what remains as perhaps the most decayed part of the inner city in three terraced houses stands a Free school, Saint Paul's School. It is run by a former university lecturer and some half dozen or so others, qualified teachers, craftsmen and social workers. The project embraces the school for fifteen to twenty adolescent girls and boys, a nursery school and an adventure playground. Most of the children are drawn from the immediate vicinity and their parents pay a nominal fee for their education. The project is supported by the City's Education Department, the Regional Arts Council and various Trusts and Charities. The craft work together with produce is sold on a stall at the Saturday street market. The school produces a Community newspaper, a float for the summer carnival and a focus for a residents' association. It is the aim of the project to assist the total community development not only to be an independent school. It hopes to improve the houses and the craftsmen on the project will be handymen but also run classes to assist people to learn how to enhance and maintain the property. They hope to encourage industry to provide work for the community, legal services, assisting social services and so on.

Like the other work described the activities, nursery school, playground, etc, serve as ends but also as a means to the end of greater community identity and greater community power to achieve satisfaction and fulfilment. So a football pitch lies alongside the railway embankment, an urban farm is planned. A piece of ground that stood as a dump for old mattresses, bicycles and other eyesores was cleared by the council through the representations of the residents. Trees were planted by them and the whole landscape community planned. Perhaps among all the many wonders of Saint Pauls, its public examination candidates at CSE, O level and A level, its camps, its superb art, craft and literature, the happiness and mature self confidence of its children, that humble piece of park stands as a symbol of the project's achievements and its aspirations.

In Canada I was told by a lecturer from the University of Calgary how as a former CBC employee he had gone to Dromhella to make a community film. The final result was essentially his film, not bad, but as he said smacking a bit of'... and as the sun sinks slowly in the west we say farewell...' However at the showing of the film some people approached him from Rosedale, a village relatively near and asked for his help to save their community from extinction. Already the school was closed and daily another sign of the erosion of the community seemed to appear. Yet despite everyone's individual concern no concerted action seemed possible or even desirable. There was a fatalistic sense of the inevitable death of the town.

The community worker, as he so regarded himself, was at a loss to know how he could turn this tide, but it was the people using his skills that won the day, not his ingenuity or dynamic leadership. The small group of concerned townsfolk requested to be taught how to use the video equipment. They did not bother with zooms, camera angles, etc. but set the equipment up in a central place and invited people to record their views about the community as moving mug shots. The film was played back and the contributor offered three choices, to erase it and retake, to erase and say no more or to keep the contribution as being a statement by which the contributor stood. Gradually the town became more involved as the news of the experiement spread and more and more contributions were gathered. The film was edited as a group decision and eventually was shown to a packed house using a number of monitors. Not only did the film create a great sense of amusement at the appearance of familiar faces but also stirred a great sense of the urgent need to act. Something like fourteen committees emerged from that meeting and the town was on the way to its later successes of lobbying government for aid and getting it, stimulating local growth through industry and building a local community pride and self-confidence. I am not sure whether television was ever used again for such a purpose in Rosedale. It had played an invaluable part in raising community consciousness, a veritable blood transfusion at that critical time. It would be good, too good, to be able to talk of how the arts flourished thereafter but what is important was how it was recognised by the townsfolk as a potential catalyst in the first place.

Telford is a new town in Shropshire, a result of the move to re-house the inner cities' demolition in the sixties, to disperse its crowded industries and create attractive environments among industrial villages of former fame in the heyday of the iron industry but now declining. The Development Corporation has laid miles of good roads, planted thousands and thousands of trees on landscaped hills and built acres of houses with social and sporting facilities in the local schools to be shared by the community as a whole. The development sounds attractive and one should not minimize its successes. Nevertheless the morale of the tenants does not reflect this optimism and the houses are already showing signs of neglect and decay. When the rain sweeps horizontally across the hills and women struggle back from the supermarkets with pushchairs, the rural idyll looks less attractive.

For the past six or so years this has been the centre for one of the most remarkable Community Arts developments. Initiated by former Senior Lecturer in Drama, Graham Woodruff, and Kathy MacKerras, already an already an experienced play leader organiser and a graduate whose studies had included community arts work, Telford Community Arts was born. A painter, a potter and a print worker were added and no doubt in time music and sculpture will be added to the impressive list of activities that one finds practised there. A regular television programme is made and relayed in the local supermarket, posters and more recently books all planned and made by community groups are published, murals exist on walls, ceramic tiles as a mural, designed made and fired decorate a school wall made by a group of mothers. The May Day celebrations are extensive and combine local talent and the work of professional community performance groups of all races. The place now exists as a venue for visiting music and theatre companies including this year the Royal Shakespeare Company. There are residents' groups, pop groups, discussion groups and a fine drama group whose productions over the past three years have emerged as of a standard to be compared with other theatre groups and immeasurably more so in that they also embrace a community's education both personal and social.

The plays arise in much the way we have described except that their coming together in the first place in a much more chancey business. The same identification of the group's concerns occurs and the material explored in improvisation. The themes have included unemployment, the case for a local hospital, a play about Iron Bridge as part of the centenary celebrations and up to the time of writing a play about family relationships as they exist as reality and illusion. The scenes are built on personal experience exchanged by the group and involve struggles with bureaucracy, the lack of facilities for infant children and their working mothers, the boredom and hopelessness that often attends such housing developments. Yet the plays have a gaiety that results in scenes of great fun and an overall sense of group strength. The players are not only people of fortitude themselves but who have gained strength through their combined expression. They also enjoy that characteristic that seems to attend work of this sort which is a remarkable ability to discuss their experience of playmaking, to articulate their view of what immediate purpose it has served and to philosophise upon the role of the theatre in the community. Nor does this come from instruction but from the persistent discussion that attends their rehearsals. The artists are engaged as actors but essentially serve the same ends as we have seen before, the improvement of the group's self-concept and self-esteem.

Nor do the plays remain merely as the performances of an amateur dramatic society. The material reflects local concerns and engages its audiences in discussion of them as well as the performance. Neither is the play allowed to appear as a mystery nor its content merely observed. Lest they sound daunting it should be again stressed that they are enjoyable occasions at whatever level the audience wishes to participate. They do reflect the joys and the vicissitudes of the community back to itself but in a coherent statement that attempts to find some meaning in their lives and communicate them.

Management

This sense of responsibility extends to the management of such Community Arts groups. The local people actually employ the artists and oversee the conduct and direction of their projects. They discuss its artistic policy and social intentions, draw up the budget and consider the final balance sheet. They are accountable to the funding bodies and to the local community. In the case of Telford Community Radio they make decisions about appointment of staff, content of programmes, purchase of equipment and so on. Nor are the boards of management composed of the usual sorts of experienced and articulate people who run a parish council or a golf club. Nevertheless, though their deliberations are not always concise they are invariably well considered and result in good and responsible government. The social process integrally associated with the arts is rarely seen happening elsewhere with such purpose and such openness.

Of course there is pettiness and frustration and all the ups and downs that arise in the traffic of human interaction. It would be discourteous to the Community Arts movement to suggest otherwise and run the risk of discrediting their efforts by making them appear incredible. Nevertheless the dedication of the workers, who rarely receive even an Equity minimum wage, and the real achievement and dignity of the communities, fills one with a sense of great optimism. The progress may seem like drops of water falling on to the stone but a lasting impression grows. Also the movement does not merely improve the lot of people, to bring it nearer the standards of living of those of us more privileged, but reveals a quality of life that very often we lack. For affluence often goes hand in hand with social isolation, people who do not know or care about their neighbours and who are equally unloved and uncared for. The lack of interest in the life of the community is reflected in the apathy shown in the polls in local elections. More often than not the advantaged share any sense of community only when their privacy or privilege seems threatened and then their manipulation of the system is as swift as it is selfish. The example of the Community Arts groups is a happy one not only because it shows the strengths and joys of community action but also how it integrates the aesthetic into the social and political. It is this process that is the link that it has with Education.

Arts and education

There is much anxiety on the part of the Arts Council to link the Arts with Education and there is a special post for one of its officers as Education Liaison Officer. The cause is a good one but it tends to look at the traditional role of education and the traditional role of the arts. Both in a way are providers, they supply information, provide access to the arts through the example of high quality performance. Nor is one attempting to decry such provision, for under its aegis many excellent things happen. It is not, however, that view of education and the arts as inseparable aspects of community life that we have discussed before. In this respect the work of the community artists not only in serving an educational end but in its pedagogy sets an example to many a qualified teacher.

Many such artists are very highly academically qualified but have turned from the traditional education institutions because they do not seem to be relevant to today's concerns. Neither their methods nor their aims seem to assist the students' personal growth and fulfilment. Nor do such institutions serve any but a minute proportion of the population. The field of education provision need is vast and yet the higher education population is so small comparatively. Furthermore these artists perceive the true name of Education, a leading out of the person, not a cramming in of information. The growth of the person, his self awareness and self-confidence, his intellect and his feelings all are vital for the true growth of each other. Also there is a rejection of education as a lonely, competitive experience and a concentration upon the individual within the group. The student is able to compare his experience with others, to learn from them and teach from what he perceives to be valuable from his own life. The immensely important task of learning to live as social man is one which he undertakes not as an abstract philosophy but as a lively reality.

Especially important is this contribution of the community to its own education. A greatly neglected area is the oral history, the songs, the proverbs – 'strategies for living' – the skills, the cures, the wisdom amassed by men down the centuries in a social and domestic setting. Too often modern day living stresses the easy come, easy go; the throwaway existence where there seems little value in a pot or a container. A switch will give light and a knob the heat for cooking and the wonder of these amenities is rarely appreciated. Neither is the wonder of that which proceeded them, for to peer at them in a museum does little to give a sense of their simple genius. The concept of progress has carried with it a rejection of former ways and the decline of the apparent value of community lore and language.

One does not advocate a simple, idyllic, rustic life, which I doubt ever existed. What however is stressed is the disastrous divorce of education from day to day life. Parents and grandparents do not feel they have any contribution to make to the education of their children beyond a purely domestic one. The engine driver or the postman have so much to pass on about their jobs and their attitudes to them. How seldom does the school exploit the rich resource that is the wisdom of the parents? They are often persuaded to part with money for a new mini-bus or such but except where their skills can directly assist in a legal, professional or practical technological sphere, are they invited to contribute to the children's education. Nor does the usual Parents' Evening that purports to be a joint venture, do much to dispel the mystification of the teaching profession. It is significant that usually parents are seen at the end of the school year when the teacher will impart what he has learnt about the child. Rarely does the teacher see the parent at the beginning of the year to seek assistance through the parent's assessment of the child.

In the play, *And Was Jerusalem* . . . where I mentioned the oral history of working relatives the students really talked to their uncles and aunts for the first time about aspects of their family history. Too often what has happened seems not to be significant in any educational sense for the child is sent to school for education. I cannot speak for the relatives for I did not meet them, but the students gained immeasurably as people, not only through the knowledge but from the intercourse, the sense of past and present. During the making of the play about the phoney war, again the recollections of parents and relatives were solicited. A young student suddenly realised that her parents' ages were then exactly those of herself and her fiance' at that time, but before her father could get married he had been sent abroad and the couple had to wait for years before the wedding could take place. The student could now identify with that agony and saw her parents as young lovers once parted by the war.

The work of Charles Parker, Ewan McColl and Peggy Seegar in the Radio Ballads where the programmes were built from the contributions of working people has affected my approach and that of a former colleague, Iain Ball now Senior English and Drama Adviser to Avon Local Education Authority. With the help of Charles Parker we were able to introduce a number of intakes of students to the wealth of wisdom, humour, poetry and drama that lies in the memory of the community. These were made into radio programmes but also influenced their style of theatre performance. The studio work of some years of students was magnificent especially Hugh Roberton's *American Civil War* a production of true originality. For not only did the students learn to listen to their contributors, and how seldom teachers listen, but also to respect the material. Thus the approach towards their reading became one of excitement and awe, feelings they tried to capture in dramatic expression and often so successfully.

This chapter may seem to be straying far away from the subject of the book, the Drama, but it is not. Drama depends upon a lively intercommunication that exists not only in words but in common knowledge. *The Conference of the Birds* that describes the travels of Peter Brook's company through Africa stresses the aim of making theatre that was not circumscribed by a particular language. Nevertheless the bond that grew was from the mimetic expression and the vocal utterance of common experience. The songs touched the heart as the comedy could make the eyes stream. The incidents symbolised the very essence of social life and the company had to relearn that experience from their contact with the village people of the Sahara. We do touch it fleetingly in drama but it needs to be fed at the source if this nourishment is not to be found only on the library shelf. A life that is a genuine community process does not allow one to lose one's roots and become a social isolate. Privacy can be respected and a great respect for individual dignity maintained. These are vital when making Drama, especially for performance, for sometimes there is a temptation to exploit and sensationalise the experience of others – the daily tabloids are a clear example.

Education is not to be contained only within the experience of a small community for it can breed bigotry and intense parochialism. Nevertheless those qualities that underpin a healthy community are the basic values from which any curriculum must draw. The classroom that so often is forged into such a community by the good teacher needs to be the world in microcosm and should open its walls to the inputs of all so through its learning it might benefit equally those who have fed it. The Drama exists as one of the ways in which the walls can come down and as with Brook's players in the desert enable people to communicate and share their life experience that often they do not regard as significant because they have never been encouraged to do so. The ultimate might be the deschooling of Ivan Illych but in the meantime the education of all, both young and old could benefit from those expansive views of the needs, aspirations and achievements of people encouraged and developed by the workers in the Community Arts movement.

Summary

The use of drama in Community Arts is studied in this chapter for its educational power. The process we have examined elsewhere is invoked but without the institutionalised pressure. Again the central concern is with the role of the teacher and his responsibility for developing confident people through the medium of their work in the Arts.

11

Drama and Education

It must be the case in the writing of most books that the tide of events sweeps like water under the bridge in copious measure between the opening paragraphs of the first and last chapters: this book is no exception. Further, and with little attendant satisfaction, the gloomy predictions made in the early days of writing have come to pass. Moreover they have been worsened by a severe decline in social and economic health such as we have not seen for fifty years. These events have affected educational planning in such a way as to have severe consequences for the arts in education throughout the decade.

It may seem a risky business to make such predictions about the future, for who would have foretold the changes in the world over the past ten years? Nevertheless we are already beginning to see the effects of recession upon public expenditure and in the whole sphere of industry. Here the traditional mainstays of British manufacturing are disappearing and the prospect of continued unemployment for a sizeable proportion of the population, including young school leavers, is a reality. Reliable forecasts suggest that this situation will worsen before we can expect to see any improvement. Certainly our standard of living will decline with lower wages, high unemployment, fewer services and high costs. The quality of our living became a neglected consideration a long time ago.

Amid all this insecurity there is less experiment, a swing towards consolidation and even retraction, especially in Education where the developments of the past twenty years are being very critically appraised. Among some there has always existed a distrust and indeed condemnation of less formal approaches to Education. Their voices are becoming increasingly seductive and are winning more support especially in the name of Accountability. The policy of 'paying our way' has resulted in the discontinuance by local authorities of many parts of their service which though they would deem desirable, they do not regard as necessary. Hence the deep inroads into the Social Services that have resulted in the closure of

Old People's Homes, Meals on Wheels, Home Helps, etc. Gone also are the subsidies on many other items that benefitted us all but especially those in need. The hospital wards stand empty though the waiting lists get longer because staff cannot be afforded to run them. The cost of medicines continues to rise so that people perhaps think twice about buying them. In education we are dismissing teachers, have virtually dismantled the school meals service and school transport in many areas. Train and bus services are being affected so that there are fewer of them and they cost more.

In this climate, Accountability thrives because, with less money to spend, it is felt that a careful consideration should determine the worthy causes. The tried and well tested seems often to be the safe investment, while the experimental or progressive must wait for better times. Though none would oppose a healthy thrift we must always be on guard against the forces of reaction, where the balance sheet is the favoured indicator of success. Also attempting to revive the glories of the past can be a fruitless task, as the present that becomes the past always seems better in retrospect.

Nor is it sufficient to say that the economic difficulties that the whole world is experiencing will get better and all will be well. Economic recovery is unlikely to create more jobs, and where apparent savings have been made, especially in public expenditure, it will be hard to persuade the renewed financing of those areas in the future. It is an old adage that if it disappears from the budget, it's dead. No, the effects of the present actions that result from a particular socio-political attitude, will remain with us for a very long time. The economic measures are the application of a particular view; a boosting of the individual as a wealth producer and a consumer sometimes at the expense of his fellow men. The philosophy is essentially divisive, for it constantly seeks to equate the recipients of its wealth supporting measures with a silent, sane majority threatened from within by anarchists, social parasites, degenerates and extremists. The dangers of such a view we are well aware of from recent history for in the name of individualism it strengthens centralised direction, reduces variety and opposes that vision of a pluralist society already discussed in the context of the Multicultural Classroom. Its concept of the product of an education system is well defined as someone whose potential to join the thoroughbreds has been recognised and rewarded by selection. His curriculum should reflect the traditional areas of learning, his absorption of which is measured by written examination. The super intelligent are taught how to think, but carefully taught what to think also, because the assessment of their thoughts stresses compliance as a virtue not challenge.

This may sound like a sixpenny revolutionary but ask many a university graduate about his experience and whether the courses actually lived up to the lofty aims of our institutions of higher education. Invariably they will confess to feeling an immense sense of inadequacy because they have lived so long with being encouraged to do better, that they can no longer believe in their own strengths. The values they invoke to assess their own worth and those around them are not only unreal but sometimes positively sick; the division of people into bright and dull, interesting and uninteresting, well read or ignorant, successful or failures, the list could go on. And such a view is not innate but is the result of a person's education. In school the children are the enemy, the despised peasantry to many a staffroom and the children know it. The sixth form invites the pupil to consider changing camps especially where his academic success has shown him to be potentially one of the elite. His higher education concludes the transformation and whereas he may not become a teacher and complete the circle by despising the children, the same division is applied to other members of society – the British workman, the workshy unemployed, the sponging council house tenant or the ignorant and over-productive immigrant.

What of those who fell in this education race to success or who did not even make the start? It has been observed that there never has been universal secondary education in Britain but that always the school and its curriculum has reflected an education programme and an ethos intended for the few. It is little wonder that the system looks so inadequate when inspected as by the recent survey. Ultimately, however, the system will be constructed for the emergence of a particular product and it is there that our gaze must be fixed. For truly creative programmes in schools will confound any compulsion towards conformity. The arts encourage people to question themselves and the society in which they live.

Where there are issues in education, therefore, we should be careful that we do not simply accept the premise of the often persuasive arguments that support the recommendations of the committees who identify them. A decline in standards of, say, spelling, should never be isolated, for the proposals for its improvement can make the total situation worse. The teaching methods may change and the lesson content, but the same unproductive relationships remain. Especially where there are implications for teacher training, and there always seems to be, there can follow more and more content crammed into an already impossibly crowded curriculum. Every teacher, it is recommended, should be numerate and literate, be familiar with science and a foreign language, religious education and physical education if in a primary school, be aware of the demands of the multicultural classroom, the conditions of British industry, the disadvantaged and slow learning child, health and safety, the law as it relates to the teaching profession, computer education and statistics, and as a headteachers' conference recommended a few years ago, a course in first aid.

Teacher performance

When such demands are taken aboard, nothing is jettisoned, so the preparation becomes more and more lost sight of. The divorce between the theory and practice becomes greater because the flexibility needed to integrate them cannot exist with such a crowded timetable and syllabus. The training does not sensitise the student teacher to what the learner and learning are about and in what ways the teacher may facilitate the process. The concentration is upon the teacher's performance and the implementation of programmes often prepared with inadequate knowledge of the children for whom they are intended and sometimes by lecturers who have no familiarity with them at all. Tips for teachers is a despised term but there is a danger that the approval of programmes at long range from the classroom can be little better. Especially an over-emphasis on the teacher's aims and objectives can persuade students that the major triumph in the classroom can be to achieve compliance. Little wonder that there can appear on inspection alarming gaps between the teacher's perception of what is happening in the classroom and those of especially adolescent pupils. Such an approach will also emphasise the professional skills and academic background the student teacher is needed to acquire. Rarely do we stress the strengths they have as people; their warmth and sympathy, their sense of humour, their attractive youthful zest, their courageous optimism that allows them to dare to venture and sometimes win and confound the doubters.

By failing to build on these qualities and strengths it often happens that the student finishes his course of training with less confidence than he started with and even having lost some of those personal characteristics for which he was selected at interview. The over anxious, strident, insensitively self-centred student on final teaching practice must be a familiar experience for many an examiner or supervisor. At best there is the danger of the shop window student who has a beautifully busy classroom, a plethora of children's work on the walls, ingenious projects and superb visual aids but somehow no heart, no sense of the child but only the adult provision. Especially in the classroom where the school serves an affluent neighbourhood the class can appear to be well taught. Nevertheless the potential of these children, even their actual strengths, remain untouched. The teacher does not know that in the class are children knowledgeable and fired by astronomy, cookery or, as in *Kes*, by falconry or the breeding of ferrets, canaries or the racing of pigeons or whippets. Often when such richness or experience is discovered, even an obsession with Bingo, the teacher realises how little he knows and how his education has been narrow and constricting not the broad expanse that it often purports to be.

We recall the wise observation we have quoted before of Joan Tough's that it is the encouraging of the child to communicate his experience as important to him and recognised as such by the teacher. Hence a visit to the zoo may in retrospect be recorded by children with barely a mention of the animals. In such a case the teacher has not to feel betrayed by the child's different perspective. Failure to show a conformity with the teacher's view can be a success not a failure of teaching performance. I well remember a head teacher of an infant school encouraging creative work through playing music. She played one of the sea pieces from Peter Grimes and asked the class what it reminded them of. Each child picked up the quality of water, though none knew the source of the piece. The teacher listened with increasing frustration and decreasing enthusiasm to the contributions of the seven year olds. When she had exhausted the suggestions she asked 'But what *animal* does it make you think of?' The children looked absolutely blank much to her dismay so she pressed them saying, 'Now I'm going to play the piece again and this time tell me what animal it makes you (sic) think of'! An obvious example of mismatch but not unusual among teachers of all age groups where the apparent open question is actually guess what's in the teacher's mind. Like the entry to heaven we need to become as little children again if we are to be successful teachers. We must be able to remember that wonderful world of the junior joke – 'What's yellow and dangerous? Shark infested custard!', the innocence of little children who can believe that the door could open and Batman enter and the immense simplicity of situations. I remember a head teacher accompanying me looking at five-year olds' painting. A baffling painting was so obvious when the child explained it was a house, for she had painted the aerial view with the roof removed. There she said was Mummy and Daddy's bedroom, there her own and the baby's, there the bathroom, with Mummy sitting on the lavatory. The Head baulked and said, 'Oh, I don't think so'. The child insisted, the Head persisted with attempts to modify. Then the child sensed the embarrassment of the adult and said with comforting candour, 'It's all right, the door's shut'!

The story is amusing but much more than that. The young child was generous and very sensitive to the teacher's needs, the teacher rather less so of the child's. Effective communication between teacher and child is not uncommon in the primary school especially at the lower end. However it often appears that as the children get older this sensitivity becomes diminished. It may be that increase of concentration by the teacher on the cognitive and the resulting destruction of integration with the affective, erodes the openess of the earlier years. Not that classes of all ages cannot enjoy such warmth and trust but only where everyone's feelings are afforded as much care and concern as their thoughts. Such an atmosphere of mutual trust ensures that real learning does take place, because none fear to take chances. A confession of ignorance or misunderstanding is not a shameful business, nor is it greeted as such. The opportunity exists always for talking things out, for through genuine questions and genuine answers, there is the expectation of all that understanding can be reached. This emerges from mutual tolerance and a sense of the rules that govern their affairs. As we remember from chapter two rules are made by equals and though there will be some external constraints, the class works essentially within its own agreements.

The teacher must never abdicate his responsibility to his class; a concern for the encouragement of learning and the skills to promote social interaction that can be used as a model for worthwhile living. This is an immensely demanding task for it demands a heightened awareness of the moment to moment conduct of the traffic of affairs and where the potential lies for the accomplishment of long term and short term educational goals.

It must by now be clear how the drama as we have discussed it, relates to this task. Its virtual present depends on just that awareness of mind, and feelings and is invoked to encourage learning. The opportunity it provides for raising interest in abstract considerations through the application of a very concrete experience is a resource in education that we have rarely begun to tap.

It is not only that drama makes a unique contribution among others that are valid and desirable. It is not that the panacea for all our social and economic ills lies in a strong diet of drama. The nub of it is that drama cannot flourish nor indeed draw breath except where the sorts of relationships and attitudes we have been examining exist. The game of drama assists the sensitising of people's awareness but it also emerges from a willingness to play, with all the responsibilities that entails.

Drama in education

We do not intend to rehearse our arguments all over again, but might find it useful to relate them more exactly to developments not only in the wider sphere of education, but to those more recent trends in the field of the development entitled Drama in Education. For while this book has been in preparation, a number of authoritive books have emerged and it may well be that they will affect thinking as strongly as did those of such pioneers as Peter Slade and Brian Way. Evidence for this view is supported by the increase of courses in the subject, particularly at postgraduate level and which carry both academic and professional awards. In-service courses for teachers also reflect this bias and especially at secondary level. The Schools Council has published two major pieces of research and interest grows internationally in the methodology associated with this increased emphasis upon the pedagogy of drama in the classroom. It may well be too early to be attempting some sort of stock taking but the urgency of the wider educational issues we have discussed implies that time for reflection is not on our side. The general approach may then be usefully reviewed and observations made on some of the strengths and weaknesses of the approach.

The history

In the 1950s and 1960s came the explosion of interest in the use of drama as an educative medium. Brian Way traversed the country running the most stimulating in-service courses as well as working with student teachers. His own book, *Development through Drama* had not been written at that time but he had assembled and ordered much of the material that was Peter Slade's *Child Drama*, and taught to that philosophy, at least in general. Slade's view was of a Child Drama as a separate phenomenon very much like Child Art that Herbert Read had identified earlier. The emphasis lay with the development of the child, especially his feelings, and offered an alternative approach to that prevailing in schools. Sometimes it could appear as positively anti-intellectual and always quite separate from Theatre and the performance as end product. It did not employ in a systematic or conscious way the work of educational psychology or sociology, the developmental stages of the child were uniquely categorised as were the observations on pedagogy.

Methods of teaching for many of us who were excited by the movement were learned from the live example; Slade's classes at Rea Street in Birmingham, later Brian Way at the Drama Centre in London. Particularly from the latter the word was spread by lecturers in teacher training, drama advisers, now being appointed in many authorities, and by school teachers. The activities that were to be recorded in his book had been well taught by Brian Way and were repeated not only nationwide but also internationally. The leader of the class would take children, or adults as a surrogate class of children, through certain experiences that would heighten one's sense of awareness and call for some invention. A theatre background assisted the teacher to structure the experiences, for the class often did not have such training and the activity had to work for them if it was to be valuable. For this form of teacher training in particular worked strongly upon the example and only then supported by some educational precepts. The analysis of the sessions involved the expression of one's feelings about the work rather than how it had been brought about or even how it was to be transferred into the classroom.

Where the centrality of Slade's philosophy was not adopted there was a casting about for some core to which the activities could be related. The most influential of these was the work of Rudolph Laban and his analysis of movement. Movement then became the basic discipline of the Drama and remained essentially teacher-centred. As mentioned earlier in the book it offered through mime to music a method of classroom control that was acceptable to many a headmaster. The strains of *The Swan of Tuonela* floating down a corridor was less likely to suggest the school's managerial instability than the screams of angry citizens of the French Revolution. Also there was a body of knowledge to be taught, skills developed and the resulting choreography observable if not necessarily assessable.

The enormous success of Pemberton-Billing and Clegg's book, *Teaching Drama* and a number of manuals that followed reflected the teachers' need for structure. Even if it were only a lesson plan, the inner structure of which was not revealed, nevertheless it served as a classroom support. Still in the guise of being severely child centred, the Drama in schools became more and more teacher dominated. Lessons purported to offer genuine discovery with open questions and real choices. The lesson plans however were absolutely clear about what was the kick of the lesson and had so ordered the events that it was achieved. The teacher, sometimes severely dictatorial in a way few teachers of other subjects would be, operated in a way that seemed non-interventionist and ready to encourage quietly the creative work of children. Nor should it be thought that with good teachers this did not happen. Especially where there was experienced classroom teachers who could graft what they found useful in the approach onto their own, some excellent things could happen. The drama became one of the means towards their educational ends for children so that its pedagogy remained unquestioned. For others where the drama lesson and its satisfactory completion was the end, its lack of wider purpose and sounder method proved a nightmare as I have recounted in earlier examples.

The Drama Survey of 1968 by the DES, often quoted in this book, was the first comprehensive account of what were the effects of all this work in schools. Although good work was seen, by far the major impression was of time wasting, aimless, teacher dominated activity, 'reeling and writhing...' The old disciplines had been abandoned, those of performance skills, and nothing put in its place. Thereafter came the Schools Council Survey 'Arts and the Adolescent' which was later to bring forth, 'The Intelligence of Feeling'. Both severely criticised the teaching of the arts in schools and often because there was simply no creative input from the children whatsoever. Indeed Witkin describes the nature of the creative process for us all but especially for those many arts teachers who have never experienced the creative. It articulated in educational terms much of the frustration that had built up but which surfaced often only as despairing cries that we must dismantle and start again. This was a predictable conference resolution especially in the early seventies. The issue on Drama in 'Education in Theatre Quarterly' and especially the article by David Clegg hastened the process. Like a reformed drunkard, he who had been the co-author of *Teaching Drama* now called for real happenings in the classroom.

In the North East Dorothy Heathcote and Gavin Bolton had been evolving their own approach to the teaching of drama. Both attached to University Education Institutes and eventually to offer advanced degrees in Drama in Education, they were firmly within the context of wider movements, especially those promoted by NATE. Their concern was with the teacher and the processes in the classroom that constituted the drama lesson. Though publicity through television and press emphasized Mrs Heathcote's uniqueness she would in her teaching persuade her students of their own strengths as a basis for the work. Her students were essentially themselves building on their own experience and relating it to theory that evolved from a process that itself confounded and rebuilt theory. What was not always transferable was the rich blend of a consuming love of literature, the strengths of the trained actress, a fine enquiring mind which seized upon the apparently common place but which illuminated it with artless candour and the fulfilling enjoyment of teaching. Paramount, though, for both these outstanding teachers is their ability to relate to their classes in a way that persuades the children to believe that the contracts they make are genuine. Especially, children discover that what they have to say is really listened to and does affect the pattern of the work.

The Schools Council's research projects, the work of the ILEA, and the links with curriculum theory of Chris Day, all have emphasised the role of the teacher. The insistence on clear aims and objectives sometimes has threatened to promote behaviourism too much, though the encouragement to evaluate carefully has maintained the debate about what is the teaching for. John Allen's book, like the man himself, is that blend of modesty over his own contribution, immense knowledge and experience of the whole field of drama and a fiery determination to see change for the better. Reading and re-reading reveals immense wisdom often expressed in a beautifully composed sentence.

Most recently Gavin Bolton's *Towards a Theory of Drama in Education* has been published and brings together in one place those thoughts about the teaching of drama that have influenced the Schools Council work, the ILEA, the Drama Board syllabuses, the Drama Panel of the CNAA, etc. It breaks new ground by its concentrated focus upon the classroom process and the emphasis upon the teacher's responsibility and participation in the evocation of drama in the classroom. The analysis of the teacher's decisions that enable him like a pilot to assist the steerage of the passage of the lesson is exhaustively laid out. Above all the emphasis upon what is being taught and what the learning outcomes, swells the tide of opinion that prefers the title Drama in Education, where drama exists perhaps to serve the ends of learning in the classroom. As with the work of the Schools Council, Gavin Bolton's book sees the aim of the work in the classroom as the making of meaning. The teacher identifies an area of class interest which at the outset is held at a level of some superficiality. The teacher takes the class through an experience using dramatic involvement that deepens this understanding of aspects of that original area of interest. Thus bank robbery as an attractive topic for exploration because of its potential violence and tension concludes with a greater understanding of its ramifications. Through a drama experience in which the teacher or the children, or both, adopt roles and turn the abstraction into a concrete present, the range of meanings associated with the topic become greater.

Formerly a charge levelled at drama teaching was that the work confirmed predjudices, through its simple stereotypes and taught attitudes that were ill-considered. The perpetual violence, hysteria and noise became, it was claimed, the class expectation, and rather than channeling the exuberance, actually bred disobedience and riot. Nor could the charge be wholly denied especially because the end of the work was its presentation. Groups of children worked on little pieces intended to illustrate a concept and then showed them if there was time. Rarely was there enough and so not only was the work not shared, but was not even discussed. The assumptions of the pieces were not challenged but often only the skills with which they were presented received criticism. The function of Drama in Education is now however seen more clearly with the teacher's responsibility well defined. His work in the classroom is the promotion of learning, as in all the other subject areas; how that takes place is the difference. The teacher uses his skill and understanding of Drama to assist the creation of opportunities for the living through of aspects of the social process.

Assessment

What will probably remain as questionable is to what extent we are able to assess the effectiveness of the learning. Without testing it would be difficult for example to discover whether attitudes had indeed changed as a result of the work. Sociometry might discover whether the social health of the group had indeed improved as a result of the group problem solving and effectively maintained relationships. Rightly such obsessive measuring would be rejected and the question asked how much do we ever really know about what has been learned? Nevertheless already among Drama teachers there exists a desire to be taken seriously so that both for themselves and the children they teach, recognition of their work is publicly demonstrated. In these days, for the teacher, this will mean the retention of the subject as part of the school's curriculum, especially where falling rolls will reduce the viability of options and when a core curriculum will not include drama. Here we revive the economic arguments and accountability that was mentioned earlier and the bleak prospects for the arts. In this context one can see what dangers can beset the teaching of drama where proof of effective learning may be sought.

In the past teachers have submitted to the pressure for the extension of public examinations to drama. Indeed some have welcomed the development as giving direction and purpose to the work. Studying drama for CSE and GCE exams has meant classes in drama beyond the third year whereas otherwise it can disappear from timetables and especially from those of the 'more able' child. The examination work confers academic respectability for the subject, the teacher, the Head, parents and children, but there is a heavy price to pay. Certainly for adherents of a Drama in Education approach, what is demanded on the examination syllabus does not appear to be what drama is about. Indeed some CSE exams appear like the requirements of an honours degree course with great emphasis laid on theatre history, dramatic literature, scenic design, etc. The practical work is aimed at developing certain performance skills and indeed the whole field of play presentation as amateur theatre is the focus for the course. This bias comes from teachers whose enthusiasm for drama has grown from involvement with amateur theatre and who feel they possess knowledge and experience that they can make available to others. The things they enjoy doing in their spare time become part of their working time too and it is not uncommon to find the drama teacher pottering about preparing for a production much as one might find people in a theatre. Nor is this to suggest that they do not work hard but it is merely perhaps a query about the appropriateness of the activity when it purports to be part of the curriculum and as such may be seen as a serious and essential part of the child's learning.

The question of distortion by examination requirements is not unfamiliar, though we should not allow our familiarity to breed contempt for that often small voice of protest that insists upon the absurdity of what passes as education as a result of them. Furthermore it is the political questions of staffing, accommodation and budget that occupy the minds of teachers and administrators and which ultimately determine the admissability of the subject. Drama teachers along with other subjects must like football managers show good results. Unlike them, however, failure results not in a change of managership but in the disappearance of the sport.

The move then towards greater comparability with other aspects of the curriculum and its teaching, though displaying in principle a greater sense of educational purpose among Drama teachers, is, however, fraught with difficulties of pragmatism. Furthermore such a move reduces the effectiveness of the argument for drama as part of an alternative approach to education. This is the most serious of all the points mentioned for whereas the other dangers can arise from expediency, a move to make drama resemble other subjects and especially in the teacher's dominance, would be a disastrous abandonment of principle.

A major achievement of the drama in schools has been where the work has been genuinely child centred. It is true that for many older children they came to discover that with some teachers the drama lesson was essentially like any other. The teacher pulled the strings in reality even though there might be a show of inviting the class to run itself. Freedom of choice and the opportunity to consider one's own interests was restricted often to the illustrative playlets that the class made in groups. Inevitably there would come the conflict of the professional position of the teacher when his encouragement of questioning brought criticism of the school management or the teaching of his colleagues. Discipline would be enforced so that the sight of a class being harangued outside the drama studio or being made to sit in silence within it is not unusual. Nor does the teacher find any contradiction in operating so, yet expecting the mutual trust and respect and equality that the group creative work demands. The discipline that is exercised by the group itself will depend on its definition of what is inadmissible. The children are the school, the education is theirs by right but their passage through the system is one that by and large is directed and controlled by adults. The fundamental position is one of benevolent despotism that easily assumes the characteristics of dictatorship if questioned or challenged. As in society at large we do not believe in the power of people to govern themselves but impose the will of others, however well intentioned they may be, in the name of management, Parliament, officers, etc.

Nor does the alternative rest solely in the activities that the class undertakes. The examination of social attitudes towards justice, freedom, religious or racial bigotry, sexual behaviour, family ties, is all very well but if the teacher/pupil relationship resembles the usual authoritarianism then social views are not challenged but merely confirmed as sacrosanct. The assumption by the teacher that his authority exists outside the sanction of the pupils, that he represents not merely a school establishment, which he might resent, but the will of the nation at large is another source of strength and comfort laid down in his training. There the emphasis, as has been described, is upon teacher performance. The language of instruction resembles the terminology of trench warfare and the task is described as the struggle between the forces of intellectual light and the powers of ignorant darkness. At best there may be a missionary zeal at worst a colonising imperialism. Rarely does the partnership assist the student teacher to seek the self appraisal of the class, to explore their concept of the whole curriculum, to be informed or sensitive to counselling and pastoral care. The teaching methods reflect the attitude of the teacher as information giver through the medium of lectures. There remains a preponderance of note taking rather than note making, a transference of information rather than its selective retrieval as part of the process of learning.

These criticisms are not the expression of what might seem a radical approach to education. They are the major criticisms of the HMI's contained in the DES report on 'Aspects of the Secondary Curriculum'. They are seen as prerequisites for a system of secondary education that could be properly termed comprehensive or to use a less emotive term, a secondary education system for all. It is seen as self-evident that the pupils must play a much more significant part in their education, with genuine decisions and real choices being made as training for the life beyond school when their responsibilities become so much greater and their decisions so very critical.

Though examining the function of the teacher in the drama lesson much of the recent work on drama in Education does not stress this co-operative, democratic aspect of teaching. There is a tendency to start from the centrality of the teacher's position and the way in which his performance both in and out of role steers the course of the lesson. The proposed destination seems to be chosen by the teacher who is able to stand back from the experience, whereas the class is not expected to plan except within the teacher's framework. Mention is often made of the way in which the teacher might switch roles to bring about certain lines of enquiry. It is never made clear whether the same freedom exists for the child. The teacher introduces the surprise element by injecting new, unexpected material, but one wonders whether the same facility exists for others. This seems to be a prize example of the breaking of a rule upheld by consensus and surely only to be accepted by a class that is prepared to accept the teacher's privileged position; the right to overrule a class decision.

At least two of the three examples of teaching in the film *Take Three* present immensely authoritarian approaches but the accompanying booklet does not seem to disagree with the teacher's self appraisal which stresses a freedom of class choice. Too heavy emphasis on teachers' aims and objectives will reduce the likelihood of genuine creative work in the classroom. Furthermore the identification by the teacher of attitudes worthy of exploration and not discussed as such with the class, can be the same old teacher/pupil situation but with a new twist. Although among the best Drama in Education practitioners this is unlikely to happen, for the egocentric bully of a teacher it can appear to sanction his bad teaching and the distortion of education. There remains the need to help all learners to the goals of self-confidence and self fulfilment through genuine discovery and the social process of negotiation. In such an atmosphere the making of meaning includes the teacher whose perceptions may be very different if he allows himself to listen, to experience real equality of opinion and direction. He must break through to a trust of the group to govern itself and for part of that group to be the adult.

The advantage of the Drama in Education movement is its preparedness to seek criticism and especially from within. It is an essential quality that its practice both illuminates theory and challenges it, so that self-appraisal is not aimed at some political justification. In the future we shall have to take care that its followers do not transform its open questions about theory and practice into closed answers. For even though theory springs from classroom operations it is easy to see in the class response what you want to see and to avoid genuine enquiry. Further the movement must take care not to become too narrowly focused upon classroom interaction and not to commit itself to the wider struggle for a child-based education. How to bring about the child's learning must never become so obsessive a teacher's concern that he neglects to question why.

In its short school life, ignoring the Tudor schoolmasters or even Caldwell Cook, drama in schools has been blown by many winds and drifted with various currents. Its direction seems more assured especially if it continues to pursue the course between appropriate pedagogic study and the magic that Ernst Fischer believed was a vital ingredient of the art.

Summary

This final chapter examines the dangers that exist for the arts in a difficult period of economic stringency. The call for Accountability can encourage an ultra conservatism and endanger moves towards a child-centred education in which effective learning, as in drama, is so crucial. The Drama in Education movement is reviewed with its strengths and potential weaknesses.

Further Reading

Bolton's book, *Towards a Theory of Drama in Education* and Wagner's book on *Dorothy Heathcote: Drama as a learning Medium,* represent the most comprehensive of statements about Drama in Education. John Allen gives a much wider survey from his experience with the Inspectorate in particular. Chris Day presents a view of drama as learning in the Upper and Middle School while the two Schools Council Surveys of Tom Stabler and Lyn McGregor, etc, serve as very valuable indicators of work across the country.

Epilogue

Schools are inescapably part of the community. Yet it is a paradox that as the child grows older and more socially aware, so the use that the teacher makes of his experience of his environment diminishes. The infant talks and writes, draws and acts his response to the life immediately surrounding him. Increasingly this experience in school becomes less prevalent, and what he learns from his home and his neighbourhood becomes less important.

This process not only alienates the child from the values that form the bases of the life of the neighbourhood, but also from the history of his own family. The labouring skills of a grandfather or an uncle, the accumulated domestic expertise of an aunt or granny, these traditional sources of learning become no longer valued and are neglected. The child is sent to school to be educated and the learning that accrues from the daily ebb and flow of life is disregarded as a formative influence.

For the large majority of our children, however, the education they receive becomes increasingly unacceptable and they leave school at the earliest opportunity. They have neither been given an acceptable preparation for life in the school's terms nor assisted to see the value and significance of their out-of-school experience.

This situation results when learning is promoted from exclusively unfamiliar sources at the expense of the child's own experience. For example, in some classrooms it appears to be held as of more consequence that a child should be able to reproduce details of the social organisation of a foreign people, than that he should relate them to his own condition and thereby widen his horizons. But where the arts are used in a genuinely expressive way, then the child's primary experience speaks with an articulation both forceful and eloquent – 'My birth was at my Aunty's on the afternoon of a Friday.'

The drama, more than any other expressive form, draws upon the player's own experience. He is required to represent the behaviour of

162

someone else, a portrayal drawn from all his encounters. So his contribution is always original and rich in detail that the player regards as significant.

This means of organising experience can be applied in most learning but is most effective where it aids insights into the life of the community and the communication of them among its members. The process is socially very healthy for it both celebrates and challenges the norms and values by which people live. It exposes what has become dead or irrelevant, what has been imposed and never integrated, what remains and continues to serve the needs of a community.

At all stages of the child's education, it is most important that he should consciously develop the skills of 'describing and communicating.' And the drama supplies the concrete example from which the child will reason and begin to ask questions about the life around him. To consolidate his understanding of the way that drama works and to what end, is to lay the foundations for the continued appreciation of the art throughout a person's life. But it remains not only as a personal recreative pastime, but as a vigorous social institution that includes in its consideration how politics, religion, work and leisure are related activities, informed by the same basic social values.

In such circumstances the theatre becomes again the Playhouse, a popular and universal meeting place for the playing of the drama game. Once more the themes reflect the great concerns of men, 'a concern for God, for society, and for the individual, as acutely mirrored on the stage as it is reflected in the auditorium.'[1] The audience and the actors – 'a living, vital communal relationship'[2] – together create the play, an affirmation of their continuing faith in social man, the ecstatic celebration of life.

So we have returned to the thoughts expressed in the opening chapter. What we seek to assist by teaching drama is the restitution of the health of our society in all its features. The claim may seem over-ambitious, but then we are privileged to work with this unique social model, this mirror of moral values. For the child it offers an enjoyable, demanding game that satisfies his needs at all stages of his growth. For the teacher it offers an extension to his teaching skills with a powerful and ordered technique, and for his pupils the opportunity to exercise, in a purposeful activity, their communication skills. Few operations in the classroom could be said to offer more.

Notes

[1] Wickham (48) page 54   [2] Wickham (48) page 54

Bibliography

Books

1 Albee, E, *The Zoo Story,* Cape 1962
2 Barnes, D (et al), *Language, The Learner and the School,* Penguin 1969
3 Bentley, E, *The Life of Drama,* Methuen 1969
4 Britton, J, *Language and Learning,* Penguin 1972
5 Brook, P, *The Empty Space,* Penguin 1972
6 Cook, C, *The Playway,* Heinemann 1917
7 Dodd, N and Hickson, W, (Eds) *Drama and Theatre in Education,* Heinemann 1973
8 Fergusson, F, *The Idea of a Theatre,* Princeton 1969
9 Fines, J and Verrier, R, *The Drama of History,* New University Education 1975
10 Furth, H, *Piaget for Teachers,* Prentice-Hall 1970
11 Goffman, E, *Encounters: Two Studies in the Sociology of Interaction,* Allen Lane 1973
12 Goffman, E, *The Presentation of Self in Everyday Life,* Allen Lane 1969
13 Goodridge, J, *Drama: Activity in the Primary School* Heinemann 1970
14 Grotowski, J, *Towards a Poor Theatre,* Methuen 1974
15 Hodgson, J, (Ed) *Drama As Challenge: Uses of Drama,* Methuen 1972
16 Hodgson, J, (Ed) *The Uses of Drama,* Methuen 1972
17 Hodgson, J and Richards E, *Improvisation: Discovery and Creativity in Drama,* Methuen 1968
18 Hodgson, J and Richards, E, *Living Expression,* Ginn, 5 books 1968-71
19 Hoetker, J, *Dramatics and the Teaching of Literature,* NCTE (USA) 1969
20 Holly, D, *Society, Schools and Humanity,* Paladin 1972
21 Holt, J, *How Children Fail* Penguin 1969
22 Huizinga, J, *Homo Ludens: A Study of the Play Element in Culture,* Paladin 1970

23 Jackson, P W, *Life in Classrooms*, Holt, Rinehart and Winston 1968
24 Kemp, D, *A Different Drummer*, McClelland and Stewart 1970
25 Kolve, P, *The Play called 'Corpus Christi'*, E Arnold 1966
26 Langer, S K, *Feeling and Form* Routledge and Kegan Paul 1953
27 Luria, A R and Yudovitch, F I, *Speech and the Development of Mental Processes in the Child*, Penguin 1971
28 Lymann, S M and Scott, M D, *A Sociology of the Absurd*, Appleton Century Croft 1970
29 Male, D A, *Approaches to Drama*, Allen and Unwin 1973
30 Martin, W and Vallins, G H *Exploration Drama*, 5 books, Evans 1968
31 Millar, S *The Psychology of Play*, Penguin 1971
32 Moffatt, J *A Student-Centred Language Arts Curriculum K-13*, Mifflin (USA) 1968
33 Moffett, J, *Teaching the Universe of Discourse*, Houghton (USA) 1968
34 Oeser, O A, *Teacher, Pupil and Task* Tavistock 1966
35 Parry, C, *English Through Drama: A Way of Teaching*, CUP 1972
36 Pemberton-Billing, R N and Clegg, J D, *Teaching Drama*, University of London Press 1968
37 Piaget, J, *Play, Dreams and Imitation in Childhood*, Routledge 1972
38 Pinter, H, *The Caretaker*, Methuen 1967
39 Selden, S, *Theatre Double Game*, University of North Carolina Press (USA) 1970
40 Shakespeare, W, *Othello*, Macmillan 1971
41 Shipman, M D, *Sociology and the School*, Longman 1968
42 Skinner, *The Technology of Teaching*, Appleton Century Croft 1968
43 Slade, P, *Child Drama*, University of London Press 1954
44 Spolin, V, *Improvisation for the Theatre*, Pitman 1973
45 Stanislavski, C, *An Actor Prepares*, Bles 1937
46 Vygotsky, B F, *Thought and Language*, MIT Press 1962
47 Way, B, *Development Through Drama*, Longman 1967
48 Wickham, G, *Drama in a World of Science*, Routledge and Kegan Paul 1962
49 Wickham, G, *Early English Stages* vols, 1 and 2, Routledge 1959-72
50 Williams, R, *The Long Revolution*, Penguin 1965
51 Witkin, R, *The Intelligence of Feeling*, Heinemann 1974

Articles, Television Programmes and Records
52 Duncan, B, 'An Uncertain Mixture', TES 30 August 1974
53 *Early Years at School*, BBC TV 1974
54 *DES Education Survey 2: Drama* HMSO

55 Educational Pamphlet 57 *Towards the Middle School*, HMSO
56 Hands, D essays in Macan, R W, (Ed) *R S of Literature*, (XII) 1933
57 NATE Conference Report, NATE 1969
58 Shipman, M D, 'Order and Innovation in the Classroom', *New Society*, December 1969
59 Williamson, H, *Children Talking*, Music for Pleasure 1224

Additions
60 Duncan: *Communication and Social Order*, Bedminster 1962
61 Newton, J, *The Journal of a Slave Trader*, Epworth 1962
62 Hunt, A, *Hopes of Great Happenings: Learning through Theatre* Methuen 1976
63 Bolton, G, *Towards a Theory of Drama in Education*, Longman 1979
64 Wagner, B, Dorothy Heathcote: *Drama as a Learning Medium*, National Educational Association 1976
65 Day, C, *Drama in the Middle and Upper School*, Batsford 1975
66 Allen, J, *Drama in Schools: its theory and practice*, Heinemann 1979
67 McGregor, L, Robinson, K and Tate, M, *Learning Through Drama*, Heinemann 1977
68 Stabler, T, *Drama in the Primary School*, Macmillan 1979
69 King, C, *A Space on the Floor*, Ward Lock 1972
70 Burns, E, *Theatricality*, Longman 1972
71 Pike, Royston, *Human Documents of the Industrial Revolution in Britain* Allen and Unwin 1966

Index